CALM AN

CALM AND INSIGHT

A Buddhist Manual for Meditators

BHIKKU KHANTIPALO

LONDON AND NEW YORK

© RoutledgeCurzon Ltd. 1994

ISBN 0 7007 0141 9

First published 1981

By RoutledgeCurzon Ltd.
Reprinted 2003
By RoutledgeCurzon
2 Park Square, Milton Park,
Abingdon, Oxon, OX14 4RN

Transferred to Digital Printing 2006

British Library Cataloguing-in-Publication Data
A CIP record for this book is available
from the British Library

Publisher's Note
The publisher has gone to great lengths to ensure the quality
of this reprint but points out that some imperfections
in the original may be apparent

CONTENTS

INTRODUCTION: WHY MEDITATE? vii

Every Evil Never Doing

I PRELIMINARIES 1

And in Wholesomeness Increasing

II THE MIND AS I r IS AND WHAT CAN BE DONE ABOUT IT 20

III THE FOUR FOUNDATIONS OF MINDFULNESS 29

And One's Heart Well Purifying

IV CALM AND INSIGHT 50

V MEDITATION METHODS 75

VI GOOD RESULTS AND BAD 105

VII DANGERS TO MEDITATION 113

This is the Buddha's Teaching

VIII THE FRUITS OF PENETRATION 122

Appendices

1 SOME QUESTIONS AND ANSWERS 138

2 A GLOSSARY OF BUDDHIST TECHNICAL TERMS ON MEDITATION 148

INDEX 151

ACKNOWLEDGEMENTS

First to Venerable Nyanaponika Mahathera, founder of the Buddhist Publication Society, (P.O. Box 61, Kandy, Sri Lanka), the author wishes to express his thanks for permission freely given to quote from the Society's translations; then to the Buddhist Society, London, for the passage from their publication *The Sutra of Hui Neng* quoted in Some Questions and Answers; and to E.P. Dutton Inc., New York for the passage quoted at the same place from their book *The Life of Milarepa*, translated by Lobsang P. Lhalungpa.

The author would like to thank two patient and hardworking typists, Liz Cook and Jean Groundwater, who though with many other things to do - *bahukiccam bahukaraniyam* - willingly gave of their time.

Introduction

WHY MEDITATE?

Every day people take so much care of their bodies, dressing, washing, feeding and cleansing them of waste matter. How much time all this takes! But how much time do they spend on their minds? When it is looked at in this way it seems that people value their bodies more than their minds, a strange thing since the mind is the interpreter of experience and decision-maker, not the body; moreover, the body lasts at most a hundred years or a little more but the mind-stream flows on bearing with it the potentials for happiness and suffering in other lives.

It is worthwhile then to spend some time on the mind every day. We take good care to feed the body wholesome food three or four times a day: the mind too should get good food - some wholesome Teaching to nourish it. The body has a wash at least once a day so that it does not become offensive to ourselves and others - but when do we 'wash' the mind? When the body is sick we search for a cure quickly so as to be free from suffering, but the mind's sicknesses - greed, aversion and delusion, are regarded as natural and we do little or nothing about them.

Then with a mind starved of Dhamma-food, scruffy from lack of a wash, sick with the three root diseases and lacking medicines, we wonder why we suffer!

To use another metaphor: when people own some intricate and expensive piece of machinery they look after it carefully if they are wise so that it does not deteriorate. The mind-heart (*chitta* in the Buddha's tongue) is infinitely more complex than the most complicated machines and requires good maintenance if it is to run well. It is more precious too and deserves some time given to it every day to ensure smooth running, which means reduction of suffering.

All these metaphors:

good food for the mind,
bathing it,
medicine to cure it,
and maintenance to keep it in good order -

point to mindfulness and meditation.

Who wants to be miserable? Who does not desire happiness? Wanting and desiring alone will not produce reduction of misery and increase of happiness. Only attention given to the mind will achieve this, for the factors which produce both these things are both found there. Neither misery nor happiness arise without causes: they cannot exist unless the causes for them are present. A wise person knows this truth and acts so that only the causes for happiness, of oneself and others, are produced. This book will explain how this can be done following a verse of the Buddha's Teaching which has been called 'the Heart of Buddhism':

> Every evil never doing
> and in wholesomeness increasing
> and one's heart well purifying:
> this is the Buddha's Teaching.*

Bhikkhu Khantipalo,
Wat Buddha-Dhamma,
Wiseman's Ferry,
New South Wales,
Australia.

---

* (Dhammapada 183).

Every Evil Never Doing

I

PRELIMINARIES

A human being has three 'doors' of communication: mind, speech and body. The practice of meditation mostly concerns the first of these which, although it controls the other two, cannot be treated apart from them. So if one wishes to set the mind-heart in order then speech and body must be trained in the same direction. All should be trained according to Dhamma, that is in the way that brings happiness and wisdom to one's own heart, as well as benefitting others. When mind, speech and body go along generally in the same direction then an absence of conflicts will be felt and some degree of peace. For this reason in this book the basic necessities for the training of one's speech and body actions are given in some detail before coming to meditation.

One who trains all three 'doors' in the way of Dhamma is a true yogi, such a person 'yokes' mind, speech and body together, so that they pull together and in the same direction. This is the way to succeed with meditation. It does of course mean that to meditate successfully each day some changes may be necessary in one's lifestyle. But one will soon find out what causes disturbance to meditation and if one values the calm and insight that meditation brings, it is not hard to set these things aside or to arrange matters so that the least possible conflict is aroused.

This chapter has been arranged so that one works from the outside inwards: we begin with friends and surroundings, continue with a brief explanation of the precepts, then follow some considerations of food, yoga and posture until we come to the question of a safe refuge. Together with the precepts, the refuges are a secure foundation for meditation practice.

1. *Friends and Surroundings*

It seems to be stating an obvious thing to say that these are important to a meditator. They should be a matter of concern to anyone who wishes to lead a good life, meaning from a buddhist point of view, doing whatever brings light to one's own heart and happiness to others while avoiding actions bringing darkness and suffering to oneself and other people. The Buddha spoke much about friends to a young man named Sigala; about many different kinds of friends who either encourage one to develop in virtue or cause deterioration. Here are some examples from his discourse.

> These four, young householder, should be understood as *enemies disguised as friends*: (1) one who *appropriates a friend's possessions* (and is marked by four things) - he takes his friend's

wealth, gives little and asks much, out of fear does not do what should be done, and only associates with him for his own advantage; (2) *one who only speaks, not does* - makes friendly statements about the past and about the future too, tries to gain your favour by meaningless statements, and when opportunity for helping you arises he expresses his inability to do anything; (3) *one who flatters* - approves of his friend's evil deeds, and disapproves of his good ones, praises him in his presence, and speaks ill of him in his absence; (4) *one who brings ruin* - is your companion when you indulge in intoxicants, such as strong liquor and fermented drinks, all of which are the occasion for carelessness, also when you saunter in the streets at untimely hours, again when you frequent (night) clubs, and again when you indulge in gambling which causes carelessness. These four should be understood as enemies disguised as friends.

But the following should be understood as *good-hearted* friends: (1) *one who is a helper* (and is marked by four things) - guards careless people, and protects their wealth, becomes a refuge when you are in danger, and when there are commitments he provides you with double the supply needed; (2) *one who is the same in happiness and sorrow* - reveals to you his secrets, but he keeps your secrets hidden, in your misfortune he does not forsake you, and he even sacrifices his life for your sake; (3) *one who gives good counsel* - restrains you from doing evil, and encourages you to do good, tells you what you do not know, and points out to you the path to heaven; (4) *one who sympathizes* - does not rejoice in your misfortune, but does rejoice in your prosperity, restrains those who speak ill of you, and praises those who speak well of you. These four should be understood as good-hearted friends.[1]

It is quite easy to know what sort of friends one has from this passage. But sometimes the Buddha described people in a less complex way:

> Not consorting with the foolish,
> rather with the wise consorting...[2]

The Commentary on this passage just to make the meaning clear quotes the following verses from one of the Jatakas (stories of the Buddha's past lives):

> Now when a man ties up with blades
> of kusa-grass some foetid fish,
> the blades of grass get foetid too:
> such is consorting with a fool.
> Now when in foliage a man
> ties up some tagara incense,
> the leaves will of the scent partake:
> such is consorting with the wise.[3]

And if any more evidence is needed that one's friends and

Preliminaries 3.

companions affect one for good or evil, a few more Jataka verses can be quoted:

> Let me not see or hear a fool,
> let me not live where lives a fool,
> let me not choose to have to do
> in verbal traffic with a fool.
> What has a fool then done to you,
> Kassapa, tell what is the cause
> why you have preference so great
> that never fool may cross your sight?
> He leads half-wittedly to loss,
> and counsels irresponsibly,
> prefers misjudgement, and, if told
> what is correct, shows restiveness.
> Nothing he knows of discipline,
> 'tis good to have no sight of him...
> Oh let me see and hear wise men,
> Oh let me live where live wise men,
> Oh let me choose to have to do
> in verbal traffic with the wise.
> What have the wise then done for you,
> Kassapa, tell what is the cause
> why you have preference so great
> that wise men always cross your sight?
> They lead wise-wittedly to gain,
> counsel not irresponsibly,
> prefer good judgement, and, if told
> what is correct, show docileness.
> And discipline they understand;
> 'tis good to have to do with them.[4]

The value of having good friends and being careful about 'fools' - those who do not even keep the Five Precepts which will be described below, should be quite clear.

Turning now to the surroundings that one lives in, sometimes not much can be done about this in which case one has to make the best of it. Other people may find that contact with Dhamma leads them to appreciate places which are fairly peaceful, if only for periods of intensive meditation practice. In Buddhist countries one often comes across the misconception that interest in meditation must mean going off as a monk or nun and staying in the forest with a Teacher. Though this is the right course for some people, such a life does not appeal to everyone. Most will find it enough to spend occasional retreats away from home and family where they maintain their meditation practice from day to day. But the Buddha did emphasize that some solitude is an important factor for successful meditation.

First he speaks of *physical solitude* - which could be attained even in an empty room in one's own house, or a shed down the bottom of the garden where the louder noises that people make can be escaped from. But a wild place in the mountains or forest, or a lonely cave

4.   *Every Evil Never Doing*

does help to emphasize bodily solitude as well as getting one away from familiar distractions.

Having achieved some physical solitude the mind has a chance of gaining mental stillness. While some may find it unnecessary to go anywhere in order to experience stillness, with most people the former is a basis for the latter. When stillness is complete and one of the *jhānas* (deep meditative states) attained, this is called *mental solitude*, the mind which is parted from the Five Hindrances. (These are: sensual desires, ill-will, distraction-and-worry, lethargy-and-drowsiness, sceptical doubt: see Chapter IV.4.a). This mental solitude, which is real meditation, not just 'meditation practice', can be used so that insight arises and with lack of grasping what could be called *'assetless' solitude* is experienced - when there is no longer any clinging to mind, body, existence, rebirth, nothing is owned because there is no self any more.

So a householder has to reconcile some degree of solitude with everyday life in the family and at work. This can be achieved by one or two periods of meditation every day, either solitary or sitting with others, one of them at least in the quiet of the early morning. And this meditation may be supplemented by intensive practice on courses at such time as these become available.

'Living in befitting places' is also reckoned by the Buddha as a great blessing. A 'befitting' place means one where the Dhamma can be practised openly without fear of oppression from either secular or religious authorities. And it means too a place where one can hear Dhamma and become inspired by it to practise further. Also it is one where a meditative monk at least visits from time to time so that one can ask questions about one's own practice as well as make wholesome kamma by supporting him. And in one's household there is little or no opposition to study and practice of the Buddha's Teaching - this is also called a 'befitting' place. It is where the Dhamma fits easily.

2. *Virtue - the Five and the Eight Precepts*

A person who trains in Dhamma cannot be unvirtuous, which for a Buddhist means at least keeping to the Five Precepts. These are beneficial training-rules laid down by the Buddha, guidelines for good conduct which are phrased as follows: 'I undertake the rule of training to refrain from
    (1)   killing living beings.
    (2)   taking what is not given.
    (3)   wrong conduct in sexual pleasures.
    (4)   false speech.
    (5)   intoxicants, (such as) distilled and fermented things, which are a cause for carelessness'.

The Buddha recommends them to people as benefiting both themselves and others. He does not command their practice but rather shows that a person who does not adhere to them is under the sway of unwholesome mental states (*aversion* in the case of the first, *greed* in the second, etc.), that he is blameable and therefore censured by the intelligent and that he brings on loss and sorrow for himself by breaking them. Whether or not this is true should be examined from one's own experience of life - and from the plentiful examples which can be found around one everywhere.

Questions are often asked about the third one, 'What do you mean by "wrong conduct in sex"?' The principle on which all these precepts are based is not different in this case: If one's actions are going to cause more conflict in one's own heart and suffering to others - be mindful and refrain from it! So if sexual pleasures are going to cause more suffering to one's own mind and body, or will bring distress to others, then they should not be done. Suffering to others obviously includes such things as rape, breaking up a stable relationship, the suffering caused indirectly to children when this happens, and of course the perversion of children. While the standard definitions of this precept refer only to the seduction of betrothed girls and adultery due to cultural conditions in India at that time, the meaning is actually as outlined here. And in India many kinds of marriage were recognized, some with and some without formal ceremonies so it would seem that sexual unions which are informal but in which both partners are steady and sincere do not break this precept. The Buddha however, spoke strongly about the evils of commercial sex and urged people to abstain from it.

Then regarding the fifth precept it is said by some that the Buddha spoke only of distilled and fermented drinks and did not mention drugs. But the word *majja* (related to English 'maddening') is found in the Pali text of the precepts, meaning intoxicants generally. Certainly the Buddha would have known of dope, hash or something similar and there are plenty of smoke-crazed, spaced-out Hindu wandering monks to bear testimony that clarity does not go along with any kind of stimulant. More is said on this in Chapter VII.

People who do not live up to the Five Precepts, breaking them often, are not reckoned as true human beings. These Precepts are the Dhamma of the human level of existence, the Dhamma which has been practised in the past and has ensured a human life this time. Keeping them one is truly human, with body and speech actions which are *humane*, not only having a human body. The Pali commentators say that one is called *human* (*manussa* in Pali) because one has a *high mind* (*uttama mano* in Pali), a pun that we can hardly reproduce in English.

Those who repeatedly fail to live up to this human standard are really asking for trouble, for if at their death they have a mind concerned with sub-human thoughts then a sub-human rebirth naturally follows. On the other hand, when the Five Precepts are practised consistently, then since no evil is done with body or speech, it becomes comparatively easier to raise up the mind through meditation. It would be unrealistic to try meditating so as to purify the mind while at the same time indulging in actions breaking these Precepts. The dangers of this have been discussed in Chapter VII.

In this life too the breakers of precepts have much to suffer through tensions and the diseases which may be brought on by them. And the Buddha remarks that they will experience these

6.   *Every Evil Never Doing*

disadvantages: one blames oneself (i.e. remorse), intelligent people also blame one, one gets a bad reputation, one dies confused, and finally when the body breaks up one is reborn in a world of suffering and deprivation. The reverse of these disadvantages are enjoyed as benefits by Five Precept-keepers.

Some people may like to practise a stricter moral code whenever they do periods of intensive meditation practice. The Buddha designed the Eight Precepts as an appropriate standard of conduct for such times. In Buddhist countries down to the present day they are usually undertaken by lay people who go to a meditation centre for some days or weeks of practice.

The first two precepts are the same as in the group of five but the third one is changed to 'I undertake the rule of training to refrain from any sexual actions'. This means that full-time meditators find that practice goes much more easily when they are not involved with sexual desires and the conflicts these produce. All the meditator's energy can be channelled into mindfulness and full awareness through undertaking the Holy Life.

The fourth and fifth precepts are also the same. The three additional ones making up eight are as follows:
(6)   food except at the right time.
(7)   dancing, singing, music and seeing entertainments, also wearing jewellery, using perfumes and beautifying with cosmetics.
(8)   a soft bed large enough for two.

A few words are needed by way of explanation. The 'right time' for food is between dawn and noon. Meditators often eat only once during this time but two small meals can be taken during the morning if one is found to be difficult to digest. The afternoon, evening and night are then free for meditation practice with a light body which makes for mindfulness and less drowsiness.

None of the things in the seventh precept are 'wrong' as depicted in puritan thought; they are just distractions away from calm and insight and so better avoided during intensive practice.

The eighth precept encourages one to sleep on a hard surface - so that sleep will not continue too long! In hot countries a rush mat on the wooden floor is the common way of sleeping. Sometimes too, people use wooden pillows, which certainly make for mindfulness when turning over in sleep!

These Eight Precepts are a reasonable ascetic basis for concentrated meditation efforts. They lead the meditator to renounce temporarily some of life's pleasures so that the mind will be less distracted. At the conclusion of that period of retreat most people undertake the Five Precepts again. Generally speaking, the Eight Precepts should be reserved for special periods and not undertaken for everyday life when keeping them will be difficult and perhaps involve strain in oneself and hardship for other people.

3.   *The Body - food, yoga and posture*

Having said something already about the body's actions and how they

Preliminaries

should be purified (by making good kamma), a few more general considerations may be added. The body cannot be 'purified' through eating this and not eating that. Whatever is eaten, the resultant solids and liquids expelled are 'impure'. However, a meditator should be careful not to eat anything which disturbs the body, by producing too much wind for instance. The writer remembers spending a Rains Residence (three months when monks stay in one temple), in southeast Thailand, an area famous for growing durian, a fruit with an extremely strong smell. Though this fruit was freely available every day at the forenoon meal wise meditators refrained from eating it. Experience had taught them that they could have durian and no meditation, or meditation and no durian!

People always ask about eating meat and fish. What has the Buddha to say about this? He has certainly said something on this subject regarding monks and nuns, so let us deal with that first. The Buddha himself and the other monks collected their food as they walked silently through the streets and marketplaces. They accepted whatever people were happy to give. According to the Buddha's instructions a monk should not ask for any particular food, unless he is sick and then only to people who have invited him to inform them of his needs.. So the Buddha, the monks and nuns too, ate whatever came their way using that food as a medicine to cure the disease of hunger. The Buddha is recorded as having eaten meat and he allowed monks to eat it if the animal providing it was not seen, heard or suspected to have been killed specially for them. In this case it is forbidden to accept it and the Buddha stresses how much unwholesome kamma donors make by such killing and by trying to offer such meat as food.

There is also a list of meats which are forbidden for a monk to eat for various reasons but the flesh of the animals listed there would be unlikely to be found in a monk's almsbowl today. When one relies on one's bowl and a silent almsround for food, as is still done in Southeast Asia today, one takes whatever comes which is good for contentment. It is not, of course, necessary to eat everything received. That depends on the monk's discretion.

Regarding householders, the Buddha laid down no rules. They have money which can buy whatever is needed. Here it is appropriate to remember how the subject of food creeps into every popular religion and often comes to occupy an important place through 'feasts' and 'fasts'. The Buddha did not want his teaching to become 'a food trip' though in fact in every Buddhist country different aspects of food have come to be emphasized, a reflection of the power of craving (taṇhā) which causes such interest in food. Through this, needs easily become confused with wants and upon the basis of craving is erected various superstructures of views (beliefs, theories, my ideas ...)

Generally it will be true that the more loving-kindness and compassion are developed the less attraction there will be towards foods involving the slaughter of animals. But care is needed here lest the vegetarian points an accusing finger at others, which is only aversion (dosa) the second among the three roots of unwholesome-

8. *Every Evil Never Doing*

ness. Another danger is becoming too much concerned about food, 'I had this combination this morning, so now I must balance it up with this and that ...' This could be called 'food neurosis' and is rooted in greed (*lobha*) the first root of evil. The body will last at most a hundred years of so and during that time even ordinary people spend a lot of time over food, buying, preparing and eating it. That amount of time should not be increased! The mind is much longer lasting - infinitely lasting if one makes no efforts towards Enlightenment and more attention should be given it, time and attention which it repays in a way the body can never do. Then there are 'holier-than-thou' attitudes regarding food. No one is holy by what they eat or don't eat! This one should be checked quickly if it arises since it is just plain conceit and so derived from the third unwholesome root, delusion (*moha*).

In the course of history words were placed in the Buddha's mouth advocating vegetarianism very strongly so that some Buddhist groups, mainly in China and Japan, are strictly vegetarian. The Buddha's wisdom can be seen if one considers the cases of Tibet and Mongolia - where a vegetarian Buddhist would have a very thin time of it during the winter!

The moderate and balanced attitude of the Buddha may be seen in the passage on reflection on food which monks and nuns bear in mind while eating. It may be chanted too. 'Reflecting carefully I use this food, not for pleasure, not for indulgence, not for personal charm, not for beautification, but only for maintaining this body so that it endures, for keeping it unharmed, for supporting the Holy Life; so that former feelings of hunger are destroyed and new feelings from overeating do not arise; then there will be for me a lack of bodily obstacles and living comfortably'[5]. It is a good reflection to do before meals and one to bear in mind as much as possible while eating.

Yoga is literally the 'yoking' of the mind, speech and body together in the same direction of harmonious spiritual development. To many people in the West now it only means certain kinds of physical exercises which, it is true, are supposed to lead on to meditation. To give the body some exercise is certainly good but this should not be overdone. It is admittedly easier to train the body than it is the mind which fact probably accounts for the popularity of both food trips and (*hatha-*) yoga. When time is limited more should be given to meditation while exercises are restricted to a few relaxing or loosening-up positions.

If hatha yoga is practised too much it tends to increase conceit about the body, which is a hindrance, not an advantage. Ability to manipulate the body in various ways seems to distract people away from the root of many problems - the mind. It is the mind that brings on many ills in the body which is why the Buddha teaches:

Dhammas are forerun by mind,
mind is chief, mind-made are they...

(Dhammapada 1-2)

(*Dhammas* are mental-emotional/physical events of short duration).

Now something should be said about meditation posture. The Buddha in his discourse on the foundations of mindfulness, which will be outlined in Chapter III, mentioned four postures: walking, standing, sitting and lying down. The first three are suitable for meditation but the last, alas, leads too easily to sleep! It may be used, however, when one is alert but rather tense. Even then, great awareness is needed to prevent the mind wandering off into drowsy states. Of the other three, standing can only be used for short periods of time, say when one has practised walking meditation for a period and then wants to be still without sitting down. That leaves two postures, walking and sitting, to be described in more detail. The details of walking meditation will be found all in one place in the first section of Chapter III.1.b, so only advice about sitting will be given here.

The first point to emphasize is that a meditator should be reasonably comfortable in whatever posture he sits in. It is no good torturing oneself into the full lotus (and the writer knows of people who were so convinced that this was necessary that they put their knees very painfully out of joint!) and then attempting to calm the mind. The body will be agitated from the beginning and no good results can be expected. Adopt a posture in which the body is erect without strain. The back should be straight and one should check that muscles are not tense. The head should be well-balanced on the neck and slightly forward. But if that inclination becomes more pronounced this is a sign of lethargy and drowsiness! The same may be said of the head inclining backwards or sideways.[6]

What should be done with the legs and feet? If one cannot adopt a crosslegged posture then use a straight-backed chair with a firm seat. Seats which are too soft are not suitable. The chair should be just high enough so that one's feet are firmly planted on the ground. And it is best not to lean on the back but to sit up straight.

A meditator on a chair though, has one disadvantage: his position is not so firm as the traditional crosslegged postures. And if he should suffer a real lapse of mindfulness then he has further to fall than the meditator seated on the ground! So it is worth an effort to be able to sit crosslegged. To do this, take a hard cushion, two or three inches thick (more if one's knees come nowhere near the ground), and place this on a mattress or folded blankets. The cushion, which should not be soft or springy and could also be made by folding blankets, is for raising the buttocks so that the knees make contact with the ground. The blankets or mattress prevent knees and ankles quarrelling with a hard floor.

The exact method of placing the legs and feet must depend on the individual. Sometimes one sees books laying down the lotus or half-lotus positions as the only ones which can be used but this is much too rigid. There are many possibilities such as: the lion-posture where the lower legs lie alongside each other on the ground with the feet partly turned up - the legs do not cross at all; then the quarter-lotus where one lower leg lies on top of another, as one sees in many Buddha-images from Sri Lanka and Thailand; the half-lotus where one foot rests sole upwards upon the opposite thigh; and full-lotus, a position to be seen in Indian and Tibetan Buddha-images, where both feet rest on the thighs. This last is the firmest and best balanced posture of all but if it is too painful then it is best to make an effort with the half-lotus. The posture used by Japanese ladies for meditation is also very suitable for some people and certainly ensures a straight back: kneel and cross the feet one on the other, above the ankles place a cushion of comfortable thickness and then sit upright. As variations for this a cushion may also be placed under the ankles, or the cushion(s) placed between the legs pointing backward without the feet touching each other. This is a very easy posture because no strain is caused by crossing limbs.

Other parts of the body: The eyes should be closed or half-closed. Some teach that only one way here is proper but this must depend upon individuals. Some feel distracted unless the eyes are closed but others experience tension when they are. If the eyes are half-closed and the gaze directed at the floor or wall a few feet away there should be little distraction. The hands are placed lightly right upon left, the fingers overlapping and thumb ends touching. No particular method of doing this is important, the hands should just be relaxed. If one is feeling tense the hands can rest upon the knees palms down but this position should not be used too much as it tends to build up tension in the shoulders. Finally, something cool may be held in the hands during very hot weather. Chinese monks traditionally use sections of green bamboo to prevent hot sweaty hands which can easily cause drowsiness.

This is also avoided by a shower or wash, especially if one is going to meditate in the early morning so that the body is fresh and relaxed. Clothes should be loose with nothing tight-fitting or constricting. They should be clean, as should the surroundings in which one meditates.

Slight deviations from a perfectly upright and balanced posture are not important and the meditator should not worry his mind thinking 'Is my back quite straight? My shoulders level? ...etc.' Straightening out the body occurs quite naturally with deep concentration and the resulting relaxation of tensions. It is not a good thing to place too much emphasis on posture, as with some Zen teachers, for this is placing the cart before the horse! If the cart is always being cleaned and polished one will be too busy to harness the horse.

Having sat in the most comfortable posture and one which also promotes alertness, one should *keep still*. A meditator should be like a massive boulder set in level ground. It is a good thing to make a resolution when one is settled into position: 'I shall not move for the period of this meditation'. If one moves then concentration is destroyed and one is back where one began. If a fly crawls across one's face, or a stray mosquito is looking for a meal, don't move! If one gets pain in the back or knees, don't move! If thoughts arise which are liable to cause agitation, don't move! Always sit out the period of time you have determined for meditation and *don't move*.

Later, in Chapter III, more will be said about mindfulness but here it is useful to note that insects on the skin are just *contact* and *feeling*, possibly *painful feeling*. Pains in the body too are only *painful feeling*. A myriad thoughts urging one to move are just *restlessness and worry*. When these things happen they should be noticed in this way and nothing should be done about them. If they continue then they may become the central theme of mindfulness until they cease. In ordinary life such things are dealt with by brushing insects off (or killing them), moving the body, and letting thoughts influence one's actions. To do nothing in these cases is to suffer, to experience something which is disagreeable. The meditator is not afraid of a little pain for he cultivates a strong firm mind, a mind which is heroic and willing to face unpleasant things.

4. The Three Refuges

Now having described preliminary matters relating to body and speech, it is time to consider a mental factor. Though many people meditate, few have a safe refuge where they can find peace and security in their own hearts. Meditation can sometimes produce fearful mental states, or gradually increase anxiety. What will a meditator do if he has no secure refuge at those times? This is why meditation should not be lightly practised, as though playing about.

In eastern countries meditators have teachers and work within a traditional religious framework. When they have confidence in their teachers and in the teaching they give, then they do have a safe refuge in their hearts. But how can this be said of someone who learns meditation techniques from some institute or person intent only on making money or gaining fame? And lack of a good refuge may even result in insanity if the fearfulness of the experience is very great. More about this will be said in Chapter VII.

A 'good refuge' was mentioned above. There are a whole range of refuges in this world, as there were in the Buddha's days:

> Many are they who seek a refuge
> on the hills and in the woods,
> to groves they go, to trees and shrines -
> men, by fear tormented.
> Indeed that refuge is not secure,
> that refuge is not supreme,
> not by coming to that refuge
> is one from all dukkha free.

(Dhammapada 188-189)

Here the Buddha points out two sorts of refuge, both of them exterior to oneself. There is refuge in the possession of material things symbolized here by the mention of land. Then there is refuge in 'sacred' groves and shrines which people thought had some special power of protection. Both sorts of exterior refuge are readily seen today where the materialist piles up possessions around himself as a refuge, and the religionist goes to some church, mosque, or temple, especially if it is to a famous place for miracles and cures. The materialist, of the two, has the flimsier refuge, for what material things last without change and deterioration? And how will those things be a refuge for him when he dies? The religionist does have a more secure refuge but a poor one since it is conceived of as outside himself. Even the most exalted conception of 'God' if thought of in any way as 'other', as exterior, cannot be called a secure and supreme refuge.

This can only be found in one's purified heart and the heart can be purified only through meditation. A meditator, to the extent that he has practised, can find some peacefulness in his heart, a quiet place to which he can retire. However, peacefulness can be upset by a change in exterior conditions or by some emotional crisis so that it is not available just when it is needed. It is little use having peace in one's heart only when things are fine!

The only secure unshakeable refuge is founded on wisdom developed through meditation. Not all meditators develop wisdom, as will be explained in Chapter VI. 'Wisdom' means the cutting, not merely overlaying, of the defilements, such as greed, aversion and delusion, the three roots of unwholesomeness (see Chapter II). When they have been cut off with no chance to sprout again, there is a secure refuge. The complete cutting off of greed, aversion and delusion, implies the penetration of the Four Noble Truths, so that there is direct knowledge of the process whereby dukkha (trouble, suffering) arises from the three roots. When they have no longer any power over one's heart, how can it be disturbed any more? This alone may be called a secure refuge.

Now, *believing* in religion and holding to a non-verifiable faith is an obstacle for the development of wisdom. Such faith is called by the Buddha 'rootless' because it is not rooted in wisdom-understanding. (See Chapter IV for the balance of these two).

The Buddha teaches one *not to believe* and that practice, which includes meditation, is essential:

> Let a wise man come who is no fraud or deceiver but a man of rectitude. I instruct him, I teach him the Dhamma, in such wise that by practising the way as instructed he will soon know for himself and see for himself. Thus indeed there rightly comes to be liberation from the bond, that is to say, from the bond of ignorance.[7]

Ignorance (of the Four Noble Truths) goes along with believing in unverifiable views and concepts. It is demolished when there is insight into the dependent origination of dukkha so that there is *knowing* and *seeing* without dependence on books, teachers, the Buddha, or on anyone. Usually such a breakthrough cannot be achieved in the various religions (including 'Buddhism') because of adherence to wrong views, which is only another way of saying 'ignorance'. But the Buddha's path contains in it the instructions for going beyond itself, for breaking attachments not only to worldly things, meditation states and heavenly delights but also to 'being a

Buddhist'.

So a person may 'Go-for-Refuge' thus showing that he is a follower of the Buddha, one who holds the Three Refuges of Buddha, Dhamma and Sangha as the highest treasures in the world, but who does not yet have a completely secure refuge. They are said to be people with a 'rooted faith', that is, a faith that does not assume anything, does not believe what cannot be verified in this life through practice. Such faith is 'rooted' in wisdom-understanding and has been illustrated by the quotation from the Buddha's words given above. It is only when people have won the final insight and are Enlightened that their refuge becomes secure and unshakeable. Paradoxically, such a person has no attachment to 'Buddhism' though the Buddha, Dhamma and Sangha are unshakeable in their hearts. They are called 'faithless' by the Buddha: they have no faith or belief; they know from penetrative insight meditation. One who believes still does not know. Here is a verse where the character of an Arahant or enlightened one is shown:

> Whoever, *faithless*, knower of the uncreate,
> cutter of links, heroic man,
> occasions' destroyer, vomiter of desires –
> he indeed is highest among men.[8]

After these preliminary remarks on refuges generally, let us take a closer look at the Buddhist Refuges.

The Buddha

> Seated serene at the sacred Bodhi's root
> having conquered Māra and his serried hosts,
> attained to Sambodhi, with wisdom that is infinite,
> highest in the Universe – that Buddha I revere.

This translation of a traditional Pāli verse tells us quite a lot about the Buddha and so may be used to describe the Buddha-refuge. First, he is pictured as seated beneath a tree which later became known as a Bodhi (Enlightenment) tree, thus emphasizing that the Buddha was an historical human being. As the commentaries point out, there would be nothing wonderful about an attainment of enlightenment were he a god, for God and gods can, according to theistic religions, accomplish most things with ease. (It is interesting to note that the devas or gods came *to ask* the Buddha questions – he did not implore their favours!) Indeed, the marvellous thing about the Buddha was that he was born, grew up and attained Enlightenment by his own efforts *as a man* showing us what it is possible for human beings to do. It is inspiring for us as human beings that he has shown the way for us to attain the ultimate perfection too, and in this life if we made the effort. Later Buddhist teachings have lost this unique flavour by emphasizing the marvellous and building upon it a theology in which the Buddha is deified. The Buddha himself would certainly have condemned such speculation.

14. Every Evil Never Doing

Views and speculations are in fact part of the serried hosts of Māra (literally, 'the Destroyer'), here meaning the defilements. They are often pictured in temple murals as demonic hordes urged on by Māra, their master, surrounding the Buddha who is seated serenely under the Bodhi-tree, this being an exteriorization of the last internal battle which resulted in the victory of Enlightenment. And that victory was not granted to him by some higher being, it was the result of his own striving so it is called *sambodhi* - enlightenment by himself. The Buddha thus cannot be fitted into such categories as 'a prophet of God to the Indians ' or 'a man with a divinely-inspired message'. For Buddhists of course, the figure of the Buddha is much more worthy of reverence than any God since he attained Enlightenment as a human being and showed the way for others to do so.

Enlightenment has been described by the Buddha in many different ways, such as the occasion when he denied possession of omniscience - of knowing everything at once, but admitted that whatever the enlightened mind was turned to, that it could know completely. So 'infinite wisdon' must be understood in this sense, that all was knowable to the Buddha though some of that knowledge was useless for practical purposes. He often described his enlightenment in terms of the Three Knowledges: of past lives, of kamma and its results, and of the exhaustion of the taints, the taints (*āsava*) being the deepest level of distortion in the mind (see Chapter VIII).

'Highest in the universe', this means that the Buddhist can see no greater Teacher in this or any other world than the Buddha, for where can one be seen who is devoid of all greed, aversion and delusion, as he was? Religious teachers may have mastered greed so that it is difficult to detect, but aversion as anger or hatred will always out, if given a chance. And anger can never be justified in Buddhist teaching by calling it 'righteous'. Anger and the violence which arises from it is always blameable and of course points out that a teacher has not yet won freedom from the defilements. As to delusion, one should examine different teachers' doctrines to see whether they preach matters which can only be accepted with faith and never verified with wisdom. If they themselves still have faith in or believe something then they are not enlightened, so how will they show a path to enlightenment for their followers? Delusion shows for instance, when the experience of dukkha is attributed to beings outside of oneself, such as to God or to Satan. A teacher who does so has not seen the causal arising of dukkha and so cannot have known the cessation of it which is Nibbana or Enlightenment.

'So you go for refuge to a teacher who is dead over 2500 years ago, do you?' might be a question asked of a Buddhist. The answer is that the more one practises Dhamma, the more the Buddha is to be found in one's own heart. When all Dhamma - virtue, meditation and wisdom - are fully developed there, then the Buddha is there. As he said 'He who sees Dhamma, sees me; he who sees me, sees Dhamma.' The refuge in the Buddha becomes stronger as more Dhamma becomes known through direct experience.

The Dhamma

> Eight-factored Noble Path for people everywhere,
> for those seeking Freedom the way that is straight,
> this Dhamma fine and subtle making for peace,
> leading out of dukkha - that Dhamma I revere.

The Dhamma is a refuge for everyone because it ensures safety. The word 'Dhamma' is from the root *dha* meaning to stand firm, be established, hold up, etc. So one who practises is upheld by Dhamma, such a one stands firm in the heart's virtues and cannot be shaken since established upon wisdom and understanding. Virtue makes a refuge because when the Five Precepts are practised the insecurity arising from breaking them is avoided. Meditation too is a refuge, a quiet, peaceful place in one's own heart which trouble and worry cannot disturb. And wisdom is the basis for the highest refuge since it tears down the structure of belief, theory and supposition which is composed of deluded mental states. The sun of wisdom then lights up the heart leaving no darkness anywhere. In this way Dhamma is a refuge for everyone no matter how little or much of it they practise. However, it becomes more of a refuge to those who practise more and the perfect refuge for those who have practised to the end.

Some people dislike this word 'refuge' saying that it sounds as though Buddhists run away from dangers, or that they are so intent upon finding a refuge in themselves that they will have no time for others' problems. But a refuge should be seen as a safe place, a place such as this transient world does not offer 'out there'. It is only by assiduous cultivation that safety can be found in one's own heart, though this does not mean that others are neglected. Dhamma-growth within by wisdom has to be balanced by the flowering of loving-kindness and compassion which is manifest towards others.

The Noble Eightfold Path which ensures this balanced growth will be outlined in Chapter III. It can be summed up by the three words which include all the Buddha's teachings upon the Path: Virtue, Meditation and Wisdom. Everyone may practise it but not everyone, in this life, is seeking freedom. Happiness in this life here and now, as well as happiness in the next and future lives, are also valid goals to strive for. But those who do want to find the ultimate happiness of Nibbana, or Freedom, it is 'the straight way'. It is called this because straightforwardness is needed in those who practise, also because as a Way it has no twistings or turnings such as are found on other paths where there are speculations, theories and theology. The Buddha likened his Dhamma to the great river Ganges which flows naturally towards the ocean, in the same way Virtue, Meditation and Wisdom flow naturally towards Nibbana. If any of these factors are missing however, it could be compared to the Ganges dammed and diverted elsewhere.

Dhamma is subtle since though it appears quite easy to understand, being expressed in the Buddha's superlatively clear language, yet the further we practise the finer becomes our understanding. The mind's powers of comprehension are refined by all three aspects of Dhamma but most of all by wisdom. This aspect of Dhamma will be considered under the heading of 'insight' in Chapter IV.

And it 'leads to peace', for when have true Virtue, Meditation and Wisdom led to conflict? It is true that self-righteous and hypocritical 'morality' has served as the basis for wars and persecutions but that is by no means 'a straight path' and those who practise it are certainly possessed of neither wisdom nor compassion. Meditation too, can make fanatics when tied to some dogmatic religion. But Buddhist wisdom makes one penetrate the facade of dogmas and dogmatic adherence, seeing them as mere supports for the ego or self. Wisdom itself can hardly make for conflict unless it is misunderstood by foolish persons as just an intellectual game, which leads inevitably to arguments and sectarianism. Dhamma, then, 'makes for peace', peace in one's heart, and peace around one. What more could be desired?

The Sangha

Right worthy of gifts is the Sangha purified,
with pacified senses, all mental stains removed,
one quality alone with which all powers won -
gone beyond desire - that Sangha I revere.

The Sangha mentioned in this verse is not the ordinary order of monks (or of nuns), but the *community* of all those people purified through the practice of Dhamma. This is the Noble Sangha and includes laypeople as well as monks and nuns. This verse is unusual though in that it does not praise all the Noble Ones - Stream-winners, Once-returners, Non-returners and Arahants - but points out only the Arahants as truly worthy of offerings.

The words 'purified', 'all mental stains removed' and 'gone beyond desire', all indicate the Arahant. No one other than an Arahant (or a Buddha which amounts to the same thing) is purified, everyone else has defilements either gross or subtle. Those defilements, which the Buddha characterizes as guests at the inn of the mind, can go, just as guests may go from an inn and be unable to return there. 'Gone beyond desire' is really only a paraphrase of the Pāli which is literally 'taintless' or 'unpolluted' (*an-āsava*) a Buddhist technical term referring to one who has passed over the ocean of craving. Since the Buddha has defined craving in terms of craving for sense-pleasures, for (rebirth in the realm of) subtle form, for (rebirth in the realm of) formlessness, 'gone beyond desire' should be understood as having no craving at all for any sort of rebirth, not merely as having no sense-desires.

All powers and abilities are won by those who are no longer tied to craving and although many Arahants had such powers (and they are not extinct even now[9]) their acquisition was never emphasized by the Buddha. He did praise a purified mind-heart and the ability to teach Dhamma for purifying others. And those who are thus purified are truly worthy of offerings bringing the donors a rich return for their

Preliminaries   17.

generosity. Other monks and nuns who are supported in this way are only worthy to the extent that they make efforts with their own training. Down at the bottom of the scale there are 'the ricebags and clothes-hangers' - idle monks and nuns who harm both themselves and, by their lack of effort, the Buddha's Teachings.

What does it mean them, to go for refuge to the Sangha? At first this is a way of recollecting the virtues of Arahants and other Noble Ones such as the venerables Sāriputta and Maha Moggallāna who were the Buddha's chief pair of disciples. Then through practice, it is becoming like them, as Dhamma becomes stronger in one's own heart. Finally, of course, one becomes a Noble One having then attained the Sangha-refuge in oneself.

There are three ancient verses often recited by Buddhists showing their devotion to the Triple Gem. Only the first of them need be quoted here as the other two are easily formed by replacing 'Buddha' with 'Dhamma' and 'Sangha'.

> No other refuge do I seek,
> The Buddha is my Refuge true,
> By the speaking of this Truth
> May peaceful victory be mine.

In this way a Buddhist shows that for him the Buddha, Dhamma and Sangha are whole and sufficient as a refuge. This means that he does not go for refuge to the devas (gods) if he is established in his practice. Others may have confidence in the shrines of the devas, their priests and holy books. He is not one therefore, who places any reliance upon mediums, seances and the information that they produce. The devas, after all, are not enlightened and may easily transmit misleading ideas. Then again, there are some devas who have wrong views, reckoning that they are permanent, or due to their conceit, in the Creator's line of business. The Three Refuges are broken if a Buddhist shows confidence in any such deva-refuge.

Others might say, 'Well, it's all the same, you know. All religious traditions make for the same goal so why be so particular about your refuges?' But this is just an indiscriminating and rather popular view which is easily shown to be inadequate. If religion is measured with a Buddhist yardstick it must, if complete, comprise virtue, meditation and wisdom. All great religions and all religious sects worthy of the name 'religion' teach the first but only some practise the second, while the third, as it is concerned with the impermanent, dukkha, and not-self nature of mind and body, is difficult to find outside the Buddha's teachings. Generally, those who follow a theistic system will substitute 'God' for 'wisdom' in the above list. From a Buddhist point of view this must mean that their meditations have led them to the direct experience of God (in the *jhāna* states, see Chapter IV) and there they have stuck; instead of developing wisdom they rely on the mystery of God. Frankly expressed, they have unknowing or ignorance when they could develop knowledge.

Buddha, Dhamma and Sangha are all aspects of Enlightenment and so most worthy of being termed refuges. Of the three, one is preeminent, that is, the Dhamma. The Buddha has emphasized this by saying[10] 'Whether there are Enlightened Ones or there are not, there is this fixed state of Dhamma, establishment of Dhamma, a law of Dhamma: All conditioned things are impermanent... All conditioned things are dukkha... All dhammas are not self'. This essence of the Dhamma (which will be treated in Chapter IV) is always true whether it is discovered or not. Then shortly before his Great Parinibbāna he addressed the monks in this way: 'Therefore, Ānanda, each of you should be an island for himself, a refuge for himself, and seek no external refuge: with Dhamma as your island, Dhamma as your refuge, seeking no other refuge.' (Long Discourses, No. 16) Finally, it is not the Buddha or the Sangha who can protect those who practise, it is the Dhamma, by that very practice. In the Buddha's words again:

> Certainly the Dhamma protects the Dhamma-practiser,
> the Dhamma well practised brings happiness to him;
> not to an evil bourn goes the Dhamma-practiser
> this is the advantage of well-practised Dhamma.
>
> (Jātaka 447)

NOTES TO CHAPTER I

[1] An Exhortation to Sigāla, Digha-nikaya 31; see *Dialogues of the Buddha*, (Pali Text Society, London), vol. III; and *Everyman's Ethics*, Wheel No. 14 (Buddhist Publication Society, Kandy).

[2] Discourse on (good) Omens (Mangala Sutta), see *Life's Highest Blessings*, Wheel No. 254-256.

[3] *Minor Readings and Illustrator* (P.T.S., London) quoting Jataka vi. 236.

[4] ibid., quoting Jataka iv. 240, 241.

[5] 'Food' in this passage is literally 'almsfood'; 'personal charm' implies slimming while 'beautification' is rounding the body out; 'living comfortably' has the interior meaning of 'abiding well in one's meditation' and the ordinary sense of 'comfortable abiding of the body'.

[6] A truly laughable picture of a 'meditator', practising his daily stint according to one of the more commercial organisations, was published by *Time* magazine a year or two ago. The man in deep 'meditation' was sprawled out in a lounge chair, head back and mouth open. Well, we are all able to meditate in this way!

[7] Majjhima-nikaya, Sutta 80, translated by Ven. Nyanamoli Thera. See *A Treasury of the Buddha's Words*, B.P.S., Kandy).

[8] Commentary: One like this has no faith, does not believe anything because he knows for himself the Uncreated, that is, Nibbāna. He has cut all attachments and bonds and is called a hero due to his fearless efforts and unshakeable heart. He has destroyed all occasions when either unwholesome *and wholesome* kamma could be made, for the Arahant makes no kamma as he has no concept of self, so he has vomited all desires, even good ones and is quite desireless. The masculine gender is used here for speaking of an Arahant because of the incident when the Buddha spoke this verse, actually about his right-hand disciple, Ven. Sāriputta. Many women have also become Arahants and what has been said here applies to them equally.

[9] See *The Life of Phra Acharn Mun - Meditation Master*. (Information on this book may be obtained from The World Fellowship of Buddhists, 33 Sukhumuit Rd. Bankok 11, Thailand.)

[10] Numerical Discourses, Threes, 134.

And in Wholesomeness Increasing

II

THE MIND AS IT IS AND WHAT CAN BE DONE ABOUT IT

When Buddhists use the word 'mind' they are using a rather inadequate English word for the Pāli *citta*, which covers both intellect and emotions, both head and heart. It is important to bear this in mind otherwise Buddhism could seem, specially to one who has only read about it and not practised, too much in the head.

So what do we mean by mind? What is going on in the present moment? A Buddhist analysis would look like this:

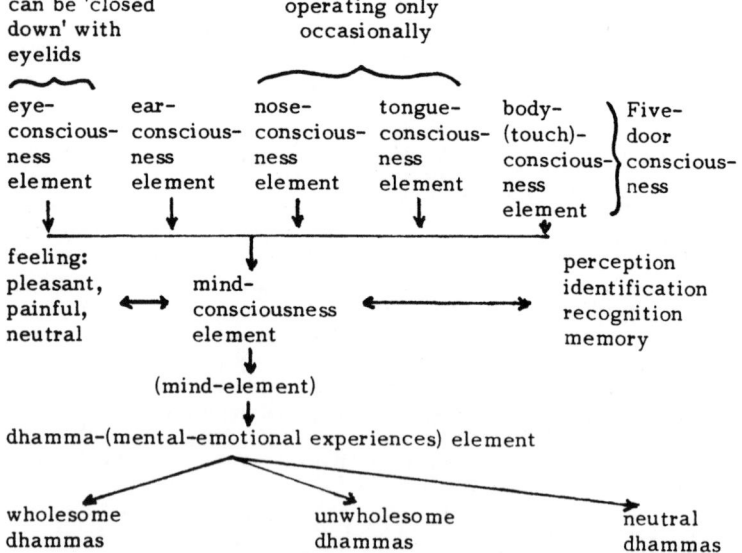

'Mind' then, may mean any one of the five sense-consciousnesses, or mind-consciousness which puts the world together using the sense impressions received and adding feelings and perceptions or recognition. If mind-consciousness is working well then the world it organizes may correspond fairly well with what is really there. But when its powers are impeded by drugs or alcohol, or by strong delusion in the case of one insane, it may put together a distorted or fearful world having little correspondence with the way things really are. The mind-element is placed in brackets as it is the unconscious or passive state which plays no part in waking consciousness, only being present in deep sleep. The dhamma-element is then the results of the various operations of the mind which may be experienced as

The Mind as it is

new decisions, that is, new kamma-making - wholesome or unwholesome, or may be the morally neutral resultants of past kamma. A mind, or rather a succession of 'minds' concerned with such highly differentiated data cannot be very concentrated. The mind is, so to speak, scattered over the wide field of stimuli and the choices presented.

A meditator by governing his choice of friends and his surroundings, as much as this is possible, can gain some restraint of the senses, so that sense-impressions do not disturb his practice when they arise as memories. His meditation practice should build up mindfulness so that the mind does not stray to unwholesome objects. Still, both in daily life and during sitting or walking meditation, the mind needs close attention, sharp mindfulness to prevent unwholesome states arising.

1. Defilements

Now what do we mean by 'unwholesome'? It is often said these days that moral judgements are personal matters, or that judgements must be made for every situation encountered. This must mean that no guidelines can be laid down for general conduct, but with this Buddhists could not agree. The Five Precepts already discussed in the last chapter are such a guideline for speech and bodily action, for they lead when well kept to the increase of happiness for oneself and other people. Is there then a guideline for mental states as well? The answer to this question is certainly 'Yes!' One can find out for oneself what is wholesome or unwholesome by experiment, though it might be a long and slow process because one may be loath to recognize *greed* which is often associated with pleasant feelings as unwholesome, besides which *delusion* does not permit one to know it as unwholesome. The latter could be compared to a fog which, when one is in it, is not recognized as a fog at all. Generally, though, people do recognize *aversion* as unwholesome because it is always associated with painful feelings, and pain is usually unpopular. Even in the case of aversion it is not always recognized to be unwholesome for it can be disguised, with the aid of delusion, as 'righteous', or even by those who are on the receiving end of it, as enjoyable.

These three - Greed, Aversion and Delusion - are called by the Buddha the Three Roots of Unwholesomeness. Let us look at them a little closer.

Greed means all forms of unwholesome or selfish desire. This may range from gross lusts connected with food and sex, to the subtle desires awakened by refined pleasures, such as classical music or a beautiful landscape. And meditators too may experience it when they grasp at some refined and blissful state which has been experienced, or when they cling to some peaceful attainment which they will not penetrate with insight. The greed, of course, is in one's own heart, not in the experience of eating, listening to music or gazing at a beautiful view. There are some actions though, which cannot be performed without greed being present, such as theft or sexual intercourse. The former is an action always blameable by society and punishable by law, while the latter is so only under certain circumstances. Greed may be recognized to the extent that it stimulates thoughts and feelings of selfishness, of conceit or the notion 'I am'. It reinforces the ego by giving it something pleasant to cling to. Therefore, thoughts of 'I want to meditate every day' or 'I wish to attain Nibbāna in this life' cannot be called selfish and are not rooted in greed. For meditation leads one to renunciation, not towards more grasping and the desire to find Nibbāna is really a desire to practise Dhamma – and by doing this desires are refined away until there is no desire – then there is Nibbāna. People whose strongest defilement is the unwholesome root of greed, 'greed-rooted' as they are called, may develop through Dhamma-practice into those who are strong in faith, for greed has the characteristic of attachment to all things in oneself and exterior, physical and mental, while faith is that attachment guided to wholesome conditions which promote growth in Dhamma.

Aversion has a similar range to greed. It may be gross, as someone in a rage, or quite subtle as with feelings of rejection and thoughts of dislike which one does not show at all. But whereas subtle greed can accompany calm meditative states even up to a formless plane of neither-perception-nor-non-perception, a moment of slight aversion can shatter good concentration. As in the world where manifestations of aversion, such as wars and murders, lead to much greater destruction that signs of greed, so it is with meditation where aversion is much more destructive. Buddhist Teachers therefore hold aversion, however it is manifest, as more blameable than greed. It can shatter the harmony of any group of people in a way that the ordinary (and socially recognized) expressions of greed cannot do. The Buddha noted that the character of these two defilements is different in that greed is a lesser fault but fades away only slowly, whereas aversion fades quickly but is a great fault because generally blameable. On the other hand, a person strong in greed may have so much attachment that he cannot train himself in Dhamma, but one who has some (but not too much!) aversion can turn this round – from seeing all the rotten things outside himself to seeing the rotten, that is, the defilements, within. It is in this way that a predominantly aversion character can change into one sharp in wisdom.

Greed and aversion are mutually exclusive. They cannot arise together though they may be alternating in some situations. Delusion, the third unwholesome root, however, is present when both greed and aversion dominate the mind. These two roots are really rooted in delusion. People would not make unwholesome kamma rooted in greed and aversion if they realised the results of dukkha which will arise, but they do not know, or if they know they choose to ignore this fact. Both not knowing and ignoring mean the presence of delusion. When we use this word to translate the Pāli *moha* it may seem that we refer to only dull mental states. These are included but are not the whole range of delusion. Under this heading are found all the following: dullness, unintelligence, distraction, worry, remorse, boredom, lethargy (of body) and drowsiness (of mind), melancholy,

The Mind as it is

depression, and sceptical doubt or uncertainty. Also closely related to delusion are fear, conceit, fantasies, and holding on to views. From the range of this unwholesome root it can be seen how powerful it is and how from it so much human suffering is born. Delusion is a great fault and fades away slowly, the Buddha says, because it is only with difficulty abandoned and so hard to be aware of. People whose minds have a strong root of delusion have to be prepared for long and persevering efforts to break it up, especially through applying the mind to examine Dependent Origination. Everyone has a problem with delusion, for it is included in the first link of Dependent Origination which is ignorance - the unknowing of the Four Noble Truths. And who is aware of even the first two of them, except occasionally? (See Chapter III).

Now that we know Mara within our own hearts how are we to tackle him? This sentence illustrates very well how tangled up with words one can become if one believes them too literally. People think in terms like this: 'I don't want to think those thoughts'; 'My thoughts should be like this, not like that'; or even 'Now I shall purify my mind through meditation'. But where is this person or owner who is somehow different from thoughts and feelings? Even with the most searching examination he cannot be found! Yet we can objectify 'an enemy within' as though somehow separate from what is conceived as one's true self or soul. So even though the next section is concerned with effort, it is not the confusion of someone who says 'I really must purify *my mind*!' Such confusion leads to confused methods being employed.

When faced with emotional problems which people do not know how to solve two methods are commonly used: suppression or indulgence. At the present time the first of these is rather out of fashion though with the pendulum swinging to extremes, it may again become popular. Certainly it should not be practised though some people are more inclined to suppress than to indulge. This is a method which employs the unwholesome root of aversion turned upon oneself. It therefore results in misery, bitterness and clinging to the very circumstances which produce these things. It is no way out of dukkha for sure!

But if suppression is not used then what is to be done? The modern answer seems to be indulgence - to 'express yourself' or 'to get it out of your system'. This can be more enjoyable in the case of greed, but what about anger? And one has to consider that actions performed again and again under the urge 'to get it out of my system' become habitual unwholesome kamma. So this way one lands in trouble too! The fruits of such kamma cannot be pleasant. This way too does not lead out of dukkha.

The only way out is by making right effort and establishing right mindfulness.

2. Right Effort

This means a balanced effort, neither too weak nor too strong. In the fourth chapter this is described under balance of the faculties. Here it can be illustrated with the story of Sona Kolivisa who, after his ordination as a monk lived in the Cool Forest:

> While the venerable Sona lived there alone and secluded this thought occurred to him: 'Of those disciples of the Blessed One who are energetic, I am one'. (He had been born in a rich family and had tender feet. After ordination he practised walking meditation with so much effort that his meditation walk was stained with blood from his cracked feet. Hence these reflections). 'Yet my mind has not found that freedom from the taints where there is no clinging ... Would it not be better for me to give up the training, return to the lower state (of a lay-person), enjoy my riches and do good deeds?' (The Buddha knew in his mind Sona's thoughts. He went to him and asked him:) 'Tell me, Sona, when in earlier days you lived at home were you not skilled in playing string music on a lute (vīna)?' 'Yes, lord'. 'And tell me, Sona, when the strings of your lute were too taut, was your lute then tuneful and easily played?' 'Certainly not, lord'. 'And when the lute strings were too slack, was your lute then tuneful and easily played?' 'Certainly not, lord'. 'But when your lute-strings were neither too taut nor to slack but adjusted to an even pitch, did your lute then have a tuneful sound and was it easily played?' 'Certainly, lord'. In the same way, Sona, if effort is applied too strongly it will lead to restlessness, if too slack it will lead to lassitude. Therefore, keep your effort balanced, penetrate to a balance of the faculties...[1]

This right effort was analysed by the Buddha in various ways, the best known being the efforts to: avoid, overcome, develop and maintain. Here is the formula from the Buddha's discourses which shows how these efforts are to be made:

> Here a monk awakens desire for the non-arising of evil unwholesome mental states that have not yet arisen, for which he makes efforts, arouses energy, exerts his mind and endeavours (=*avoidance*). He awakens desire for the abandoning of evil unwholesome mental states that have arisen, ... (=*overcoming*). He awakens desire for the arising of wholesome mental states that have not yet arisen, ... (=*developing*). He awakens desire for the continuance, non-corruption, strengthening, development and perfecting of wholesome mental states that have arisen, for which he makes efforts, arouses energy, exerts his mind and endeavours (=*maintaining*). This is called right effort.[2]

This passage shows the Buddha's methodical approach to right mental effort. Such effort does depend upon the development of mindfulness already attained while it strengthens mindfulness still further. Wisdom is also developed by quickly spotting unwholesome mental states and making the effort to overcome them.

The Great Teacher propounded five methods that a meditator could use for changing unwholesome to wholesome mental states:

The Mind as it is

(1) replacement of unwholesome thoughts by wholesome ones, as a carpenter might knock out a coarse peg with a fine one;
(2) considering the danger of unwholesome thoughts and how they lead only to suffering, just as a young woman or man would loathe a dog's carcase hung round the neck;
(3) forgetting and non-attention to unwholesome thoughts, as a person not wanting to see something would shut his eyes or look away;
(4) giving attention to the quieting of unwholesome thought-formations, in the same way that a person running might think 'Suppose I walk'; walking might think 'Suppose I stand still'; standing still might think 'Suppose I sit down'; sitting might think 'Suppose I lie down' - so going from a grosser to a subtler pose;
(5) forcible suppression of unwholesome thoughts, just as a strong man might seize and beat down a weaker one.[3]

The first four methods can be generally recommended for clearing away unwholesome thoughts in a wholesome manner. In the case of the first one, suppose thoughts of lust dominate the mind, then right effort should be made in this way: 'This body of mine is just a bag of bones, so much skin enclosing flesh and blood and an assortment of bodily parts'. When one looks at one's own body in this way, the lust for another's body disappears. If the trouble is rather aversion then try bringing in some thoughts of loving-kindness. This is more difficult however when angry and it is better to consider the danger of those unwholesome burning thoughts, thus using the second method in considerations of this sort. 'Thoughts of anger burn me now, they antagonize others and they have a terrible fruit of dukkha (suffering) in the future. I want happiness, not dukkha! Why then be angry?' - and so on. Not attending to the unwholesome thoughts should be used especially when they are strong and by their strength tend to make that type of unwholesome mind continue. Quieting them, the fourth method, can also be translated as 'tracing back the source of those thoughts' which does actually quieten them. For while one is considering how, step by step, they developed, the mind becomes calmer. Whenever the wholesome factors of mind such as effort, mindfulness and wisdom to investigate become dominant, unwholesome mental states fade away. Unwholesomeness cannot stand in the face of wholesome mental states, just as darkness however long it has dwelt in a cave instantly vanishes when a light is brought in. Wholesome states of mind are stronger than the unwholesome. It is for this reason that training oneself in Dhamma is possible.

The last method should only be used when the other four have failed to dislodge powerful unwholesome thoughts. Even then suppression should only be used if it is guided by wisdom-understanding, not the usual sort rooted in aversion.

These five methods should be borne in mind and used whenever appropriate. Unwholesome mental states should not be permitted to continue in the mind and it is not called 'making an effort' if one thinks that they are only impermanent visitors at an inn and will soon go of their own accord! The continued dominance of unwholesome states results in the mind becoming steadily darker, as a windscreen which is never cleaned becomes steadily more opaque with spattered mud. Using another simile the Buddha said:

> Do not disregard evil, saying:
> 'That will not come to me' -
> for by the falling of water drops
> a water jar is filled:
> the fool with evil fills himself
> gathering little by little.
>
> (Dhammapada 121)

3. Daily Mindfulness

If one thinks when sitting down to meditate 'Now I'll be mindful' after being generally unmindful all day then meditation will not succeed. Making an effort with the mind leads on to greater mindfulness in everyday life. What this means is paying attention to whatever one is doing while doing it, without having a barrage of distracting thoughts going on at the same time.

If you walk down to the corner shop to buy something, try *only walking while walking*; not thinking while walking, or gazing about distractedly while walking, but walking composed, mindful and fairly much at peace within. If you travel regularly on public transport and know exactly where to get off, try *only sitting while sitting*, not staring out of the window at the dull suburbs streaming by, or distracting oneself with books or newspapers. Do you ever stand in a queue? Then practise *only standing while standing*. Other simple jobs should be tried out mindfully - one recent writer suggests *washing the dishes while washing the dishes* and cutting the lawn, cleaning the car and sweeping the house could be suggested too. Mindfulness grows with practice and more complex work in which maybe other people are involved can be accomplished mindfully after beginning with the simple things.

People have been known to object 'But I want to get away from the dishes! I'll be bored trying mindfulness with such dull routine!' Well, that is just it - one must make an effort to overcome boredom (rooted in delusion) and not escape into fantasies (more delusion). Those who wish to be proficient on the piano have many hours of exercises to do first. It is no good saying 'They're boring!'. The mind too has to be exercised in the same way and it is only in everyday life that one can be mindful. What other time do you have?

Patient effort and mindfulness bring certain good results which as everyone desires them may be listed here as a kind of incentive.

(1) One does not have accidents or make mistakes.
(2) One is not plagued with a bad memory.
(3) One accomplishes well whatever one does.

Mindfulness brings greater awareness so that accidents become less likely to occur - and of course even if they do a mindful person does not make excuses ('It slipped'). Memory improves greatly so that

The Mind as it is

time and money are not wasted on slips of the mind. And then things are done well be a mindful person. Unmindful people when painting the house spatter paint all over the windows - and leave it there. Mindfulness means carefulness, accuracy and attention to detail. A young bhikkhu in North East Thailand made a back door out of local hardwoods for one of the huts in the monastery. He had no training as a carpenter yet when he came to put the door together - and it was panelled - a knife could not be inserted into its joints. This is a good result of mindfulness.

We are told in the commentaries that the Buddha spoke his discourse on the Foundations of Mindfulness in the land of the Kurus (around modern Delhi) because the people there were diligent in applying mindfulness to their everyday lives. Here is an incident that illustrates this point.

... In that land of the Kuru people, the four classes - bhikkhus, bhikkhunis (nuns), laymen and laywomen, generally were earnest by nature in the application of the Foundations of Mindfulness to their daily lives. Even servants, the very lowest, usually spoke with mindfulness. At wells and in weaving sheds meaningless talk was not heard. If a woman asked of another 'Mother, which Foundation of Mindfulness do you practise?' and got the reply 'None at all', then the woman who replied was reproached in this way: 'Your life is shameful; though you live, you are as it dead!', and she was taught one of the foundations. But if on being questioned she said that she was practising such and such a foundation then she was praised thus, 'Well done! Well done! You are really one who has attained to the human state! It is for the likes of you that the Perfectly Enlightened Ones have existed!'[4]

NOTES TO CHAPTER II

[1] Translated by Ven. Nyanaponika Mahathera in *Anguttara Nikaya, an Anthology* Part II, p. 56 ff., Wheel No. 208-211, B.P.S., Kandy.

[2] Translated by Ven. Nyanamoli Thera in *The Life of the Buddha*, published by B.P.S., Kandy 1972 (reprint 1978).

[3] These five are from a discourse of the Buddha: see *The Removal of Distracting Thoughts*, Wheel No. 21, B.P.S., Kandy.

[4] Translated after Soma Thera in *The Way of Mindfulness*, B.P.S. 2518/1975, pp. 35-36.

III

THE FOUR FOUNDATIONS OF MINDFULNESS

The Buddha clearly pointed out the direction of his teaching on meditation with these words: 'This path, namely the four foundations of mindfulness, goes in one way, to the purification of beings, to the surmounting of sorrow and lamentation, to the disappearance of pain and grief, to the attainment of the true way, to the realisation of Nibbana'. Seldom has the Buddha been so emphatic about the means to be used as here. Indeed, some translators render the beginning 'This is the sole way for the purification of beings...' And when one considers the subject of this emphatic utterance - mindfulness, the reason becomes clear, for what good Dhamma can be practised without mindfulness?

If one would like to practise giving and generosity, the necessary basis for the growth of compassion, how can this be accomplished without mindfulness? Surely one will forget to give, the chance will go and the time will pass, all because of unmindfulness! Or perhaps one wishes to keep pure the precepts that one has undertaken but then through lack of mindfulness one breaks them when there is a temptation. Or one tries to be a meditator but mindfulness is poor so the mind is confused with dull trance states or endless distractions. While such a 'meditator' has little calm and one-pointedness, he will have no insight-wisdom at all because the latter only arises with strong mindfulness. So nothing good can be accomplished without mindfulness while the meditator to succeed needs it firmly established in the mind.

The Buddha has outlined the range of mindful practices in a Discourse called 'The Foundations of Mindfulness' of which only a summary of some aspects will be given in this chapter. Here no practical instructions will be given and for these the reader should consult Chapter Five. More detailed information upon these foundations of mindfulness may be obtained from other works.[1]

Now what of the four foundations of mindfulness? They are the Contemplations of: body, feeling, mental states, and mental events. They may be dealt with in this order used by the Buddha which progresses from the grossest aspects of a 'person' to the subtlest of experiences.

1. *Contemplation of the body*

The body is the most solid and material thing which is regarded as 'mine' and 'myself'. This attitude strongly rooted in ignorance, produces much sorrow and trouble (dukkha) when the body shows quite clearly that it is *not* 'mine, as in times of disease, decay and death. Insight into not-self should begin with the grossest attachments and then proceed to the more subtle, hence the Buddha begins with the contemplation of the body. However, even one of the exercises from this contemplation alone is enough to reach Enlightenment and it is not necessary for everyone to practise all aspects of the four contemplations. The individual exercises, such as those on mindful breathing or feeling, are suited to different characters and to different periods of development. It is here that the importance of a Teacher can be seen.

Under this heading only three exercises, the most practised ones, will be described: Mindfulness of Breathing, the Four Postures, and Full Awareness. Some further practical details relating to them will be found in Chapter Five.

(A) MINDFULNESS OF BREATHING.

Here is a bodily process which goes on day and night from birth right up to death, an ideal subject for contemplation for it can never be left behind! It can and does become finer and more subtle with increased concentration. (Compare the laboured breathing of someone who has run some distance with the fine breath used when concentrated upon a book, for instance). This indicates how breath and mind are closely related with fine breath indicating a refined state of mind. This is the principle used when one practises mindfulness of breathing, quite a natural development with nothing artificial or forced about it. One should not determine to hold or control the breath - just let it come and go naturally. This is in marked contrast to various 'yogic' breathing techniques which do stress such control.

The naturalness of mindful breathing is emphasized by the Buddha in the first four 'stages' of the process. Actually, it would be more practical to call this first tetrad a method for cultivating mindfulness. It begins with the awareness of 'breathing in a long breath' and 'breathing out a long breath' - the sort of breath that one is likely to have at the beginning of the practice. As far as possible, one should not think 'I am breathing in a long breath...' but just let there be the bare awareness of the process. As concepts of 'I' and 'mine' are the basic source of trouble one does not want to strengthen them by meditation! The second part of the first tetrad consists of the awareness 'breathing in a short breath' and 'breathing out a short breath' - the kind of breathing that is a result of some concentration. The meditator will find though, at the beginning that long and short breaths are mixed up but so long as there is awareness of their difference the breath will tend to become finer and shorter.

Though this way of developing mindfulness and concentration begins with attention given to a bodily function and is therefore counted as part of contemplation of the body, it does not end with it but progresses through the other contemplations.

Under contemplation of feeling, the next tetrad, the breathing passes through four more stages beginning with the experience of rapture (*pīti*). When the breath has become very fine it may stop, or appear to, while the body is almost unnoticed. The only bodily thing

Foundations of Mindfulness

which is easily noticeable is rapture into which the breath seems to have been transmuted. This rapture can be experienced in many different ways, such as tingling and waves or currents, even flashes like electric shocks which may travel up and down the spine or along the limbs. (More about this will be said in Chapter IV.2 and Chapter VI).

The refining process continues when the rapture gives way or changes to bliss (*sukha*), the former having physical manifestations while the latter is purely mental-emotional. Then comes experience of the subtle activities of the *citta* (mind-heart) in connection with the breathing process and the calming of these activities.

The next tetrad on the contemplation of the mind consists of stages where a meditator experiences, gladdens, concentrates and liberates the mind. These first three groups of four stages all concern the cultivation of calm, while in the last tetrad concerning mental events the meditator develops insight: contemplating impermanence, contemplating dispassion, contemplating cessation, and contemplating relinquishment. Though this scheme of stages of development is found in the Buddha's discourse on Mindfulness of Breathing, and was much elaborated by later teachers, it does not follow that all who practise this way of meditation have to experience every stage. Much depends on the individual.

With this one exercise alone a meditator can experience both calm, and insight and reach the heights of insight practice where Nibbana is known. Indeed, it is said that Gotama himself used this method when he was striving for Enlightenment and that through mindfulness of breathing he reached the full-final attainment, a great encouragement for the beginner! Moreover, this practice is suitable for all sorts of people with different types of defilements. Generally everyone has some distraction during meditation when thoughts, words and pictures break up mindful attention. This is the medicine to cure the disease of distraction! And it is a gentle technique and with most people unlikely to produce any fear or danger, so it is quite suitable even if one has no Teacher nearby. More upon methods in the fifth chapter.

(B) THE FOUR POSTURES

The whole life of a human being is spent in these four postures, changing from one to another when there is too much pain or discomfort (*dukkha*). They are: walking, standing, sitting and lying down, so this is another exercise where the subject cannot be left behind. The subject of mindful awareness here is very straightforward because one has always to be in one of these four, still it needs lively mindfulness to maintain concentration as the material of the exercise is only sparse. It involves cutting down all activities to only awareness of the body's posture and seeing how this is changed.

While walking (or running) there should be mindfulness only of 'going', not 'I am going' and the same applies to the other three postures. Sitting is just the bare contact of the body on the meditation cushion, standing, just the pressure of the body on the feet and their contact with the earth, while lying down is the bare attention given to the body's contact with the bed. This exercise is not aimed at developing calm though a certain amount of it will arise, its objective is insight (*vipassanā*) through seeing only changing postures, not a self who changes them, or through knowing the inherently uncomfortable, indeed painful, nature of this body. While moved every so often these pains can be escaped from and ignored but once the body has to remain still, as seated in meditation, then the pain or dukkha can be noticed easily. If any posture has to be maintained for any length of time, not only sitting, the same thing will be observed. A hiker who finds his country walk twice as long as he expected knows all about dukkha, so does one who has to stand long in a queue, while a comfortable chair would become an instrument of torture if one was compelled to sit in it for hours on end, and anyone in hospital who has to lie down for weeks or months has also a plentiful acquaintance with dukkha. Only the fearless investigation of dukkha leads out of it. Trying to pretend that it does not exist only meshes one in more troubles!

This is another exercise which can lead all the way to Enlightenment. All who have experienced this complete Awakening have done so in one of the four postures, though they may not have used this method, with, according to Buddhist tradition, one exception. Indeed, there is a riddle sometimes asked among Buddhists 'Who reached Enlightenment in none of the four postures?' - a seeming impossibility! The answer is that Venerable Ānanda Thera, the Buddha's chief attendant, did so. One night before the First Council which was to recite and codify the Buddha's Teachings, Ānanda made great efforts, determined to experience Enlightenment before its opening. He spent most of the night doing walking meditation and then standing awhile, but finally, tired out he decided to rest a little and then continue his efforts. Going into his hut he started to lie down and experienced the enlightenment of Arahantship when his feet had left the floor and his head not yet touched the pillow!

(C) FULL AWARENESS[2]

The last exercise was for those having more constant mindfulness and bright wisdom, while this one, an expansion of it in some ways, is more suitable for people who have some trouble maintaining mindfulness. The text mentions the following activities when one should be fully aware: moving to and fro, looking towards and away, flexing and extending the limbs, wearing the outer robe and other robes (for lay people this means putting on, wearing and removing clothes), carrying the bowl (one's plates and mugs of food and drink), eating, drinking, chewing and tasting, evacuating the bowels and making water, walking, standing, sitting, going to sleep, waking, talking and keeping silent - which just about includes everything one does with wholesome states of mind.

This exercise in full awareness has been analysed by the

Commentaries into four aspects, the first of which is Full Awareness of Purpose. It is common to find people engaged in doing things which will not lead to the goal they have in mind. That can only be arrived at by the sort of activity appropriate to the intended result. One who practises full awareness, therefore, should question himself before starting any activity whether it will in fact lead to the desired result. In this way, by a pause for careful consideration, one can save oneself a great deal of energy. This is as true in meditation as in mindful activity in everyday life. And whether the one or the other, one's goal should not be lost sight of, nor the means by which one will attain it. In the Buddha's Teaching the attainments of three goals have been praised by him: happiness here and now (attained by practising as much of the Dhamma as one can in this life); happiness hereafter (the bliss to be experienced in a future life, probably the next one, as a result of having made good kamma in this and previous lives); the Supreme Happiness of Nibbana, or Enlightenment, *bodhi* (won by the complete practice of virtue, the attainment of deep meditation and the penetration of all ignorance with the light of Dhamma). If one wishes for any of these three goals, one's aim and purpose must be rightly directed. This leads us on to the consideration of the second aspect.

Full Awareness of Suitability emphasizes how the means must be suitable to the goals intended. Here one should consider whether one's means are in accordance with Dhamma or not. If not, then the three goals of Dhamma cannot be attained. At times one hears people say that their goal is the Supreme Happiness to be attained in this very life. But when one looks at their surroundings, their ways of doing things and at the efforts they make to practise, it can often be seen that their purpose and their means do not match. Such people need to know of this aspect of Full Awareness so that they may measure more accurately their actions with their goals. When these two aspects are well practised they lead quite naturally to the third aspect: Full Awareness of one's 'field' of meditation.

Like the first two, this applies both to formal sitting or walking meditation practice, as well as to mindful everyday life. It is easy enough, as any meditator knows, for the mind to slip off the meditation subject and in less than a moment to be far away. This kind of Full Awareness prevents such a thing, it steadies the mind constantly with the meditation subject. In daily life too the meditation subject can be kept going by an earnest meditator, particularly where there is something to repeat to oneself. More will be said about this later but here it may be noted that it is common in Buddhist countries to use words like 'Buddho' (the Enlightened One) and 'Araham' (the Supremely Worthy One), while other words in English like 'peace' or 'love' may also be used. Once such repetition has started it can go on almost automatically yet with mindfulness, so that the mind cannot be dragged all over the place by various sense stimuli. In this way the subject of meditation is not abandoned even in everyday activity.

But is may be that a person is drawn to the 'dry', insight-only approach in which case he has no one particular subject since the four kinds of mindfulness, of body, feelings, mental states and mental events, all become meditation. By the use of the Full Awareness of one's field of meditation, the mind-heart then never departs from Dhamma since everything done is known mindfully while the roots of wholesomeness are strengthened. Again, as with the other aspects, this one leads to the last –

Full Awareness of Undeludedness: this is the perception that what is usually regarded as 'mine' or 'myself' (my house, my family, my body, my thoughts, my views...) are not mine because no owner actually exists. While this perception only comes to full fruit at Enlightenment still it is an aspect of Full Awareness that can be cultivated in daily life, especially when 'possessions' whether human, animal or inanimate, die, decay, get lost, stolen or just wear out. There are plenty of examples of this happening all the time but what is one's reaction? Does one reject change and decay though they are inevitable and perhaps become angry? Or maybe one becomes depressed and sad? This is the way of the world, not the way of Dhamma. If one would cultivate the latter, one should frequently bring to mind the Three Characteristics of Existence – impermanence, dukkha and not self, which will be more fully described in the next chapter. Their very nature is undeludedness and the more that they are brought into focus by consideration of them, the more the mind-heart is purified of delusion – and the greed and aversion which often accompany it.

So this exercise too leads all the way from rather 'mundane' mindfulness connected with ordinary details of living, to the full awareness of the completely undeluded mind of Enlightenment. Still, the 'mundane' details should not be neglected in favour of more supposedly exalted activities for many have attained Arahantship while engaged in mindful contemplation of everyday things. Such was the case with the boys Samkicca and Pandita who knew the ending of their defilements when their heads were being shaved to become novices. And lesser attainments too come from Full Awareness, as with Princess Ubbarī who while squatting on the privy saw the maggots wriggling below and attained deep concentration (*jhāna*) based on penetration of unattractiveness.

In the light of what has been said here upon the first contemplation, it may be seen perhaps how true is the Buddha's saying 'Mindfulness, I declare, is helpful everywhere'. And this truth will become clearer from consideration of the next three contemplations.

2. Contemplation of Feeling

After the body, feeling is the next most obvious component of a person. Feeling does not mean the complex of ideas and sensations expressed by the word 'emotion', it means simply pleasant, painful or neutral feelings, regarded apart from the likes and dislikes which may arise based on them.

The Pāli name for feeling – *vedanā*, also tells us that we should *know* them, that they should be a source of knowledge for us. (The

Foundations of Mindfulness

same root is found in English wit, witch and the archaic verb 'wis' - to know, though here it has lost the experiential-emotion meaning of the Pāli vedanā). Why should the feelings be known? Because they indicate very clearly what should be avoided and what should be cultivated. When well-known with mindfulness the bare feelings of pleasure, pain, and neither one nor the other - neutral feeling, provide much useful information for the meditator.

How does pleasant feeling come into existence? The Buddha explained that one of the senses is first stimulated, in this way - 'Dependent on *eye* and *forms eye-consciousness* arises. The meeting of these three is *contact*, with *contact* as condition there arises *what is felt as pleasant or painful or neutral*.' (The same process applies to ear and sounds, nose and smells, tongue and tastes, body and tangibles, mind and mental objects). The usual way in which this process develops is then through *recognition* (saññā) referring back into the memory for some relevant information, then *decision* - the bare intention about what should be done based on memory and feeling, which is reinforced by *craving* and followed by *thought conception* and *discursive thought*.

At this point though we are only interested in the first part of the process tracing the arising of feeling. There is not much to be done about *eye* and *forms*, except that the restraint of the eyes (and other senses), when this is both possible, will make for non-conflict. Eyes (and other senses) are a part of this bodily collection which though a product of mother and father is also called kamma-produced form, since its development and maintenance depends partly on past kamma. The *forms* one sees partly depends on past kamma too and one's evaluation of them is also coloured by kamma made already. *Eye-consciousness* does not arise in the absence of the previous two, while *contact* depends on all three. This is the 'touch' of the form upon the eye while eye-consciousness is operating. On the basis of this contact arises feeling. Now this is interesting as many people would assume that thought comes before feeling. This would amount to supremacy of the head and rational thought over the heart and feelings. But the Buddha shows - and a meditator should investigate, that feelings arise first and so colour the nature of the thoughts which come later.

It is indeed fortunate for meditators that feelings do arise first since this provides a point where mindfulness can be applied and the process towards craving be cut off. In the scheme of the twelve-linked Dependent Origination which the Buddha spoke of so many times[3], 'dependent on feeling arises craving' is one very important link. Feeling here means the feeling arising due to past kamma - and the links preceding it are kamma-produced too, that is they are all kamma-results or the fruits of kamma. But craving is the making of new kamma, a strengthening of the whole process of birth and death and all the dukkha associated with it. So if mindfulness of feeling is developed then craving is checked. Let us look at this in more detail.

Nearly everyone has the experience of having suffered some pain or injury and then at least feeling disgruntled and perhaps out of sympathy with others. The painful feeling comes first and the anger, the activated second unwholesome root, later. This may be contained within oneself or it may be expressed in gestures, actions and words. And it is common too either to repress the anger or to express it as these two ways are the only ones known to most people. But the Buddha teaches mindfulness of feeling as the way out of these two extremes. Be mindful of the painful feeling, just knowing it as 'pain, pain', or wordlessly contemplating it. Anger and aversion have then no chance to arise so that they do not have to be suppressed, nor does one have to make the bad kamma of expressing them. Painful feeling is then the indicator pointing out a possible occasion for aversion. It is a warning signal and should be duly noted!

Here the arising of painful feeling and aversion has been explained first, partly because most people would be only too glad to be rid of both, partly because it may be more conspicuous for some than pleasant feeling. As we pointed out already it may not always be possible to be rid of the feelings of physical pain but it is possible in this way to be rid of the mental painful feeling with all the aversion that is often produced.

Not everyone is so keen to rid themselves of greed for this first root of unwholesomeness is activated through pleasant feeling arising, and who does not enjoy pleasure? Mindfulness of pleasant feeling, just as 'pleasure' or 'happy feeling' will limit or check subsequent greed without recourse either to indulgence or suppression. And there are some situations in lay people's lives where such limitation or checking of greed is also very useful – so that one does not get embroiled in relationships, for instance, which will only bring complications and sufferings. Pleasant feeling then, is also a warning light which should be heeded, so that greed does not increase.

Then there is the feeling tone present most of the time in this life and which because it is neither painful nor pleasant is hardly thought of as feeling at all. Yet this neutral feeling is also a pointer of great importance and it actually points to what is stronger and with greater range of unwholesomeness than greed or aversion, that is, delusion. When neutral feelings arise one is unaware of them, one does not know them clearly, and this is to say that one is *ignorant* of them. Delusion is just a part of ignorance (*avijja*), for it implies *deluded* states of mind centred on the idea of self which are *ignorant* of the process of dependent origination. But the aim of a Buddhist should be penetration of all deluded states and ignorance with the light of insight-wisdom.

The Buddha therefore advised that the inclination towards greed in pleasant feelings, the inclination towards aversion in painful feelings, and the inclination towards delusion in neutral feelings, should all be given up. More about this will be said in the next section of this chapter.

3. Contemplation of Mental States

This contemplation is again more subtle than the last with mindfulness here observing states of mind as arising and passing away. A word should be said here about the differences between the English word 'mind' and the Pāli word *citta*. First, this term usually includes feeling, which is the basis of emotion, so 'heart' is also within the meaning of citta. In the context of this contemplation however, there is less emphasis on the emotional side as feelings are dealt with separately. Still, greed, aversion and delusion and their wholesome counterparts non-greed, non-aversion and non-delusion can all be deeply rooted and involve unwholesome and wholesome emotions.

Second, 'mind' in English is used in the singular for one person and one only speaks of 'minds' with reference to many people. In Buddhist tradition though, when speaking on the level of conventional truth, one person may be said to experience many cittas, many 'minds' which change according to interior and exterior stimulation. Of course, this is seeing things in a deluded way since insight-wisdom reveals no 'person' who owns or experiences different 'minds'. This will be examined in the next chapter.

From the ordinary point of view and of a person just beginning meditation, there is an observer who knows things about his own mind. Indeed, the Discourse on the Foundations of Mindfulness bears this out by saying: 'Here a bhikkhu knows the lustful citta as lustful citta' and so on. That is, a later citta or mental state knows a former citta as lustful. This means that the later mindful citta is aware of something already fading or gone, for the unwholesome, in this case lustful citta, cannot co-exist with the wholesome citta based on mindfulness and wisdom. But as this is practised repeatedly the 'person' conceived of by unwholesome states of mind, actually by the unwholesome mental factor of conceit, steadily dissolves away until there is just the mindful arising and passing away of these minds or cittas.

The first three items under this contemplation are the roots of unwholesomeness, greed, aversion and delusion. These three have already been mentioned twice under the heading of Defilements in Chapter Two and in the previous section of this chapter. As they occur at the beginning of the contemplation of mental states this emphasizes the link between feelings and mental states while outlining a more subtle way to be aware of them. This way of contemplation used alone requires an alert and attentive mind for only 'bare bones' of mental states are mentioned in the Discourse, the most important being the two contrasted groups of roots. There is no other information given by the Buddha about this contemplation so aside from the rather few people who will be able to practise in this way, it will be best to use this method just when necessary. Either during meditation or during daily life if one is mindful enough, one may, if troubled by one of the unwholesome roots, say to oneself 'Mind with greed ... with aversion ... with delusion' according to what has arisen. This much of bare attention, which may have to be repeated on some occasions when the defiled mind is strong, is very helpful in removing the trouble.

This method is far superior to other ways in that no conflict is involved, only truthful 'spotting' of the unwholesome mental state.

At the beginning this involves words, giving a name to the unwholesome, but later this is not necessary as the mindful mind quickly spots the trouble-maker wordlessly.

When contrasted with more usual methods this way of mindfulness shows its superiority. Maybe one has tried arguing an unwholesome mental state out of the mind - like trying to pry loose a tenacious shellfish from the rocks! Or the method of ignoring it and pretending it is not there like the ostrich's legendary tactics in the face of danger! Or one justifies it by saying that everyone has greed, aversion and delusion - they are natural, so nothing's to be done about it, as though a person with a terrible disease should exclaim 'It's natural' and though the cure was available yet do nothing. Such attitudes cannot even alleviate the distress brought about by defilements, let alone lead to a cure.

Nothing more need be said here about the unwholesome roots but the wholesome roots which have hardly been mentioned as yet should be treated more fully.

Non-greed is the first of them. This word looks strange in English for we do not have the tradition of using negative-looking words for positive qualities. In Pāli this is a common practice and it does have some advantages. By the use of such a word one may contrast it neatly with greed thus making an easily remembered pair but more important perhaps, the range of meaning of such a word becomes greater. In this case, non-greed covers generosity, selflessness and renunciation, factors which are essential for any kind of spiritual growth. Generosity is not only a matter of external giving, for whatever is done with body and speech has first been planned or determined in the mind. Even sudden acts of generosity are prompted by the mind. And in the mind thoughts of generosity should be encouraged at the right time. If of course one's meditation is directed towards mindfulness of breathing or upon loving-kindness, then such thoughts are intrusive but they will not bring deterioration and should just be noted as 'mind of non-greed' and the attention returned to the meditation subject. They can then be taken up after the meditation period at such time as is appropriate.

Generosity is the soil out of which loving-kindness and compassion grow and flower. We shall have more to say about them below. Meanwhile it may be noted that generosity always involves other people, while renunciation, the other component of non-greed does not necessarily refer to others. It is true that in giving a gift one has to have some of the spirit of renunciation in one's heart, without it one could not let go and the gift could not be given. But renunciation extends not only to one's possessions but also to this body and mind also regarded as one's own. In this respect renunciation is not a forced and artificial 'giving up' of pleasures, which is often only a thinly-disguised repression, it is a natural letting go because of lack of interest. As one grows on any spiritual path renunciation occurs naturally due to increasing maturity and decreasing craving. So 'renunciation' is not a word to fear, nor to bring up pictures of a specially ascetic life, it will just manifest as spiritual growth takes place though of course it can be increased with more intensive

Foundations of Mindfulness

practice under a good Teacher.

Awareness of the presence of non-greed can be a cause for its growth, though in training oneself with mindfulness it should not be expressed as 'Oh, see how generous I'm being!' - which is just liable to increase conceit! Notice of such wholesome qualities should be limited to a bare attention - 'the mind of non-greed'. And in this way which is not egocentric at all perhaps a great deal of rapture or bliss may arise, which in turn could be the basis for deep calm, and that for the arising of insight. There are many examples of this in the Buddha's Discourses and Commentarial Stories.

The second root of wholesomeness - non-aversion - also covers a wide range for it means both loving-kindness and compassion. The systematic cultivation of the former will be explained in Chapter Five. Here we shall only say something of the range of these two important terms.

Metta or loving-kindness is love which is both purified and selfless. By 'love' in English too many different though related things are meant and because of this confusion occurs. The Pali language though has three or four words which cover the range of 'love' so that one may distinguish better what is worthy of cultivation and what is not. *Kama* is the first of these meaning at its widest sensual desires and the pleasures derived from them, but in this context having the meaning of sexual desire and the pleasure derived from sex. Into such desire there always enters as a mental-emotional factor, lust. This is classified as a defilement, an unwholesome factor of the mind, as it causes trouble, brings in its train dukkha and leads to an increase of mental-emotional turbulence. It is of course the basis for the continuance of this world but that cannot be made the excuse for indulgence beyond the bounds of the Third Precept (see Chapter I, 3). This erotic 'love' *by itself* is selfish for one desires only pleasant feelings. The other person is not considered, while people outside of the couple concerned are not even thought of at that time. So the range of kama, erotic or sexual love, is very narrow and egocentric. It can of course be practised with metta and made the vehicle for the increase of loving-kindness but the latter is not necessarily present with sex. Next up the scale comes *sneha*, attachment, especially the sort found in families where there is not much real warmth though the people are stuck together (the literal meaning of *sneha*) by sentimental affection. This may be a kind of bargain arrangement where father gets home cooking for instance, while mother gets security. But it may exist also in the absence of sexual relations among other family members when it is better known by the word *piya*, dearness. There is a certain degree of concern for others within the family in this attachment and dearness though this may not exclude harming others exterior to the group who stand in the way of this degree of 'love'. Therefore it can be called selfish to a limited extent since one's own aim comes before that of others even though it may have the guise of consideration for them. It is a better basis for the cultivation of loving-kindness than *kama*. *Metta* stands contrasted with these aspects of love as it is completely selfless and chooses the welfare of everyone. In *metta* there is no leaning on others, no getting something from others, no manipulation of them for one's own ends, there is not even sentimental affection for them. While *kama* and *sneha* will produce both physical and mental sufferings, *mettā* can never result in such a thing, its fruits are happiness for one who cultivates it and a harmonious environment too.

Now that we have some idea of the meaning of *mettā*, what is its range? It begins with oneself, that is to say, one has to have a reasonable amount of love and respect for oneself before one can act with *mettā* towards others. The aim with others is to extend to all the same quality of selfless love, not only to human beings but to all animals and to beings who are usually invisible. This is to have a heart free from enmity towards any living being, for anger and enmity never produce anything good while loving-kindness never brings any harm. We shall see how loving-kindness can be extended even indefinitely through meditation in the chapter giving practical details (Chapter V).

Coming now to compassion (*karunā*), a sympathy with others' sorrows and active steps to help them, this cannot be developed unless there is a basis of loving-kindness. Compassion as an aspect of the root of non-aversion may arise during meditation when the sorrows of other living beings come to mind. Then one may be deeply stirred by this memory and if this happens it can be the basis for a great deepening of calm, or for profound insight to arise. If it leads to such a deep stirring of the purified emotions then it is excellent but it should not result in depression, nor of course in the desire not to see suffering which is just the opposite of compassion. It may be used sometimes when the mind has become too sluggish and complacent as a kind of medicine to cure this sickness. But at other times, compassionate thoughts may be rather a subtle distraction, perhaps even an escape from some dukkha which should be faced in oneself.

These two, loving-kindness and compassion, comprise the root of non-aversion. The Buddha has highly praised both of them and emphasized how they are fundamental for leading a happy life, for growth in Dhamma, and most essential for the meditator.

If he is to win the highest, then attention has to be given to the growth of non-delusion. This is another name for wisdom, the development of which will be dealt with in the second part of the next chapter. Wisdom (*paññā*) includes clarity of thought - what is called the intellect, but it goes far beyond it. Thus a clear and intelligent appreciation of Dhamma both through learning and Buddha's words by heart and from reflection on them, is the basis for penetrating their truth by meditation practice. Undeluded states of mind arising during meditation should be strengthened by giving complete attention to them. They will concern three things: impermanence, dukkha or not-self (the last one includes voidness). The next chapter reviews them in detail.

Foundations of Mindfulness

4. Contemplation of Mental Events

This includes the most subtle aspects of Dhamma, the fleeting 'events' or dhammas that arise and pass away. Mindfulness needs to be very acute to detect this process of change and there are few people therefore, whose practice begins with these exercises. It is more common to arrive at them after having practised one of the previous contemplations which sharpen perception and provide a base for this one. An example of a person who used this method without any need to practise (due to past excellent kamma), was Venerable Sāriputta, the Buddha's right-hand chief disciple. When he heard the first two lines of this verse he became a Stream-winner:

> Of dhammas arising from a cause
> The Tathāgata has told the cause of them
> And of their cessation too
> Thus the Great Samana teaches the way.

Here the Buddha is called both the 'Tathāgata' - one who has reached reality, or literally, 'gone to Thusness', and 'Samana' - one who has made himself peaceful. This is the teaching of Dependent Origination also found particularly in this contemplation of mental events. We can see this in the phrasing of the first exercise in this contemplation.

(A) THE FIVE HINDRANCES

These are hindrances first to the attainment of deep meditation states (jhāna) but also hinder the arising of wisdom in everyday life. They are as follows: sensual desire, ill-will, lethargy and drowsiness, agitation and worry, and sceptical doubt. More about them individually will be said in the next chapter.

The meditator should contemplate them in this pattern:
(i) when present know 'sensual desire (etc.) is present',
(ii) when absent know 'sensual desire is not present',
(iii) know how arising of unarisen sensual desire comes to be,
(iv) know how abandonment of arisen sensual desire comes to be,
(v) know how the future non-arising of abandoned sensual desire comes to be.

This contemplation is aimed at only insight so here with bare awareness the meditator gives his attention only to *presence, absence, arising process, cessation process with effort,* and the *process to use in future for abandoning the hindrances.* That is, one should become thoroughly aware of the hindrances themselves, and also of their absence. One should know very well what sorts of thoughts or other stimuli set off the arising process. Though defilements need no effort their cure does require this, so one should be quite clear about how much effort and in what way it should be made. When this is known for certain then the method to use in similar situations in the future is not in doubt. The simile of a doctor may be used here. He knows when a disease is present by the symptoms displayed and he knows too that in their absence that disease is not found. And he is well aware of the sort of conditions that give rise to that disease as well as the medicine that must be used to cure it. Lastly, he knows that if that medicine is used in future it will also be appropriate for this disease. The meditator is his own doctor curing the diseases of the mind-heart as they become manifest.

While at the beginning these contemplations may use a certain amount of words in the mind, to be effective they progress to a silent knowing of all this, where there is no labelling of 'presence', 'absence' and so on. This mind that just knows without words and concepts is fine and subtle but still far from the enlightened state. It is still a conditioned mind, not the Unconditioned (or Nibbana). But this general process is the way to approach the Unconditioned because, first, it quiets all words and concepts (even Buddhist ones) and second, related to this, the idea of self is excluded and only dhammas or 'events' are noticed.

The five hindrances are important for all meditators even though they may not take up this exercise, therefore they are treated at greater length in the first part of the next chapter which deals with the development of calm. From their inclusion in this contemplation which is only for insight their great importance can be judged. Such contemplation as outlined here will not be effective for most people unless considerable calm has been attained already. Without this, the mind is too scattered and coarse and the fine and subtle 'events' of these hindrances will not be seen.

(B) THE FIVE AGGREGATES

The same may be said of this exercise where the five component groups into which the Buddha analysed what is called 'a person' are regarded in the light of their arising and passing away. The five aggregates are: body, feeling, perception, mental formations, and consciousness. Not much need be said about the first of these but it is important to note that it is not to be viewed as 'my body' but just with bare awareness as 'body'. The three sorts of feelings have been discussed already and so need no further words. 'Perception' means the process of recognition and identification and involves memory. 'Mental formations' are thoughts which may or may not be volitional, that is, they may be new kamma (for kamma *is* volition or intention), or they may not be as with formations which are the results of past kamma. 'Consciousness' means the six sense consciousnesses, of eye, ear, nose, tongue, body (touch), and mind.

This is the totality of the human being, this is what the idea of 'person', usually seen all-of-a-lump, dissolves into when viewed with mindfulness. Other notions are all included here, such as soul, Self, and God. They are mental formations too, supported by other aggregates such as perception, consciousness and feeling. They are all just conditioned things.

All these conditioned things, all five aggregates have to be noted according to this pattern:

Foundations of Mindfulness 43.

(i) such is body (etc.),
(ii) such is arising of body,
(iii) such is passing away of body.

The moments in which each of these exist are very brief. Usually our lack of mindfulness and wisdom means that we view ourselves 'all-of-a-lump' and so do not see the arising and passing away of the aggregates, moreover the concept 'I am' blocks insight. When this exercise is done then the person dissolves (and with it the unwholesome mental states on which this concept is based) and insight arises into the conditioned nature of all phenomena and when this occurs then the abandonment of the concept of self becomes possible, as the Buddha said, like putting down a great burden and not picking up another. (Chapter IV. 4).

The five aggregates need not be analysed in this exercise, for if one did so then it would lead to a confusion with other contemplations such as those of body and feelings. It is sufficient just to view the arising, existence and passing of them with bare attention. While this exercise too may involve some words in the mind at the beginning, later they disappear and only the process of arising and passing away is seen.

(C) THE SEVEN FACTORS OF ENLIGHTENMENT

These seven factors - mindfulness, investigation of dhammas (events), effort, rapture, tranquillity, collectedness, and equanimity, are pointed directly at Enlightenment, provided that they are developed in a balanced way. It should be noted that mindfulness heads the list. No Enlightenment therefore without highly developed mindfulness! All of them may be present to some extent even among those who are just beginning meditation practice but they are very subtle by the time that they can be considered as enlightenment-factors. A meditator could easily develop them off-balance, for instance, by becoming addicted to rapture or tranquillity at the expense of mindfulness and effort and this is where, again, the advice of a Teacher is most helpful. Something more on balance of mental factors will be said in the next chapter.

After noting the leading place given to mindfulness here, one should be clear about the meaning of the second factor, investigation of dhammas. This does not mean the Buddha's Teaching or Dhamma but refers to events (dhammas) arising and passing away in the meditator's mind. It is this factor in particular which leads directly to insight (vipassanā). What is to be investigated - impermanence, dukkha and not-self, of all the dhammas, will be the subject of the following chapter's second part. It is worth pointing out here that faith and confidence do not form part of the essentials for Enlightenment, while investigation of what is actually going on does. Faith or confidence is a factor already established by good practice of virtue and meditation because one has seen the benefits of these things for oneself. At this advanced level of practice the meditator is going beyond faith - to knowing and seeing things as they really are - and he will then be rightly called 'faithless' (Chapter I.5).

44.   *And in Wholesomeness Increasing*

If these factors are not cultivated, either through the practice of this exercise or some other way, then Enlightenment cannot be expected to happen. Although the moment of Enlightenment, the Paths and Fruits, are not conditioned, for the experience of Nibbana is the Unconditioned Dhamma, yet the way has to be clear for it to occur. It is as though there were a track up a mountain strewn with boulders and earth slipped down from above, then in order to get to the top someone clears and levels the path till eventually he is able to climb to the summit and get a perfect view. These factors of enlightenment can be compared to clearing and levelling the path. The only difference between this simile and the experience is that no one is there on the summit when there is perfect view! For more on this see the second part of the following chapter.

(D) THE FOUR NOBLE TRUTHS

These truths are both the basis for an understanding of the Buddha's Teaching (when they are known as Right[4] View) and the topmost height of penetrating truth (when they can be called Perfect[4] View, or No View). They are;
  The Noble Truth of Dukkha
  The Noble Truth of the Causal arising of Dukkha
  The Noble Truth of the Cessation of Dukkha
  The Noble Truth of the Practice-path leading to the Cessation of Dukkha.

There is no space here to describe them in detail as they have been the subject of many works already[5]. The most important thing to notice about the Truths is that they are verifiable.

That the first one is verifiable scarcely needs much comment as the Buddha describes it in these terms: 'Birth is dukkha, decay is dukkha, disease is dukkha, death is dukkha; grief, lamentation, pain, anguish and despair are dukkha; being united with what one does not like is dukkha, being separated from what one likes is dukkha, not getting what one wants is dukkha; in brief, these five grasped-at aggregates are dukkha'. Everyone has some experience of dukkha as a truth of this life, the most obvious forms of dukkha being the grossest ones - decay, disease and death. But as one becomes more aware of the unsatisfactory nature of experience the trio of 'being united with what one does not like, being separated from what one likes, and not getting what one wants' comes more into focus. Lastly, the dukkha inherent in body and general to all the aggregates because they are 'grasped-at' as being self or soul, this dukkha becomes easier to see. And all the five aggregates are impermanent. From what is impermanent no real security can be found. When there is no security then anxiety and fear are manifest. And these are manifestations of dukkha.

Dukkha should not be translated 'suffering' for although it includes suffering there is plenty of experience in the world which is pleasant *but is also impermanent* and therefore, dukkha. It would be ridiculous to say that it was suffering! English has no word with a range of meaning wide and deep enough for dukkha.

Foundations of Mindfulness 45.

On the level of deep mindfulness practice, it is not the grosser aspects of dukkha that are reviewed. These have already been investigated maybe through the contemplation on the body and the contemplation of feeling. The dukkha to be seen when contemplating dhammas is the dukkha associated with the five grasped-at aggregates or that which is related to impermanence.

The second Noble Truth shows how dukkha comes into existence through grasping or craving. The Buddha's description of this truth is as follows: 'It is that craving that gives rise to repeated birth (lit. 'again-being') and bound up with pleasure and lust ever finds fresh delight, now here, now there, that is, craving for sensuality, craving for being (or existence), craving for non-being (non-existence)'.

Mindfulness is the only way to become aware of this craving or grasping which is all the time fraught with fear. We are well enough acquainted with the anxieties which are always bound up with the possession of valuable things. They have to be locked up and guarded in various ways, and even then they may be lost to us - with experience of dukkha due to attachment - by accidents or just by decay. But generally this body and mind are not included among the list of treasured possessions - indeed, the way they are often treated one would think that they were worthless! Yet they occasion more dukkha through their changefulness than any exterior thing.

The unwise person who does not know Dhamma finds more and more dukkha from attachment to the five aggregates but for a mindful person investigating the aggregates with wisdom dukkha and impermanence are seen as the source of liberation. What is an enemy to the fool is a friend to the wise!

Craving has been defined in terms of what it grasps at - sensual experience, existence or non-existence. With mindfulness the constant grasping at sensuality - a grasping which paints an 'I', self or soul into the picture all the time, can be seen in terms of arising and passing away, till there is no experiencer any more. Also the craving for existence which is usually only experienced at the time of death, or when this life is threatened, is to be seen as craving for dukkha. Even rebirth in the most exalted Heavens as a deva (or 'shining one') is bound to involve dukkha to some extent for even there experience is impermanent. The craving for non-existence is mostly seen in those who have had more dukkha than they can bear. They have reached despair and crave for an end of it all. This may lead to suicide, or to wrong views that there is no more existence after this one. But an end cannot be made by just craving for it as the Buddha points out - 'But this cannot be got by mere wishing; and not to get what one wishes is dukkha'.

Craving for sensual experience and craving for existence spring up from the unwholesome root of greed, while craving for non-existence is based on the second root - aversion. The third root, delusion, gives energy to both.

When craving is seen in this light, as the source of dukkha, its causal arising should be investigated so that it can be abandoned. Generally one who practices this exercise will be concerned with the subtler ranges of craving gradually removing the sticky threads which wrap around and cling tightly to even good meditation results. This causal arising should be investigated in terms of the following process:

(i) eye, ear, nose, tongue, body and mind are delightful and pleasurable things in the world: there this craving arises and takes root.
(ii) sights, sounds, smells, tastes, touches and mental objects ...
(iii) eye-consciousness, ... mind-consciousness ...
(iv) eye-contact ... mind-contact ...
(v) feeling born of eye-contact ... feeling born of mind-contact ...
(vi) recognition of sights ... recognition of mental objects ...
(vii) decision regarding sights ... decision regarding mental objects ...
(viii) craving for sights ... craving for mental objects ...
(ix) thought conception for sights ... thought conception for mental objects ...
(x) discursive thought for sights ... discursive thought for mental objects are delightful and pleasurable things in the world; there this craving arises and takes root.

One may understand this process intellectually but that will not cut off the craving. Only meditation and mindfulness will do that!

The third Noble Truth, of the cessation of dukkha, has been defined by the Buddha in terms of Nibbana: 'It is the complete fading away and extinction of this very craving, its forsaking and giving up, the liberation and detachment from it'. When the cause is given up then the effect does not occur: this is the general principle though in this case 'the cause', an entanglement of ignorance (of the Four Noble Truths), craving and grasping supporting the self-concept which itself rests on craving, conceit and views, with the outgrowths of greed, aversion and delusion, is scarcely a simple one!

The above ten stages of what are actually the four mental-emotional aggregates - consciousness, perception, feeling and mental formations when applied to Cessation, the Third Truth, show how this comes about:

(i) eye, ear, nose, tongue, body, mind are delightful and pleasurable things in the world; there this craving may be abandoned, there it may be extinguished, - and so on, down to -
(x) discursive thoughts for sights ...

Before, in discussing the three Roots of Wholesomeness, we touched on Non-greed in its aspect of renunciation. Here we can glimpse the deepest form of that renunciation when all bases for selfhood are abandoned after seeing that all possibilities for being or existence are bound up with dukkha. For this to happen the third root of the wholesome - non-delusion or wisdom, must operate at full strength and upon the basis of Great Mindfulness. It is only when these two, mindfulness and wisdom, go hand-in-hand that Enlightenment becomes possible. Then they are compared by the Great Teachers in Thailand to two halves of a wheel which follow each other round irresistably so that Great Mindfulness supports the insights of Great Wisdom, which in turn makes for the continuity of

Great Mindfulness.

The fourth Noble Truth is the insight in the Way. The Eightfold Path is a marvellously practical way to train oneself but insight into the truth of that path is not won except on Path-moments. (A description of them will be given in Chapter Eight.) At that time oneself becomes the Path, indeed the Arahant who has seen the truth of non-self never deviates from the Noble Path, his whole life is the Noble Path.

There is no space here to describe this path in detail and it will be listed instead with brief explanations based on the Buddha's words.

(Wisdom Section:)

Right View	=	(i) Four Noble Truths, (ii) Kamma and Results.
Right Intention	=	of renunciation, loving-kindness and compassion.

(Virtue Section:)

Right Speech	=	refraining from lies, slander, harshness and gossip.
Right Action	=	refraining from killing living creatures, taking what is not given, wrong conduct in sexual relations.
Right Livelihood	=	refraining from any livelihood in which one can only harm other beings.

(Collectedness Section:)

Right Effort	=	to restrain the mind from evil and to cultivate all wholesome qualities.
Right Mindfulness	=	Four Foundations of Mindfulness.
Right Collectedness	=	the four jhānas (see Section 2 Part 1 next chapter).

So it is by means of mindfulness that the Buddha's Teachings may be verified, even those which are called 'peculiar to the Buddhas', that is, the Four Noble Truths. These are the essence of Dhamma and all the rest of his teachings can be understood only in the light of them. While they look straightforward enough, their practice is not so easy and their realization needs great effort. So one should not think that because the words describing them are quite easy to understand that they have no profundity. The more practice is done, the more profound becomes one's view of the Noble Truths. The Buddha's wonderful wisdom may be seen in the way he was able to describe in readily understandable terms practice and realization that goes beyond words. He did not experience the Four Noble Truths in the words that we have them now but he was able to describe them clearly in such a way as would guide those who wished to practise towards Enlightenment. These descriptions of deep mindfulness

48. *And in Wholesomeness Increasing*

practice in the Contemplation of Mental Events (dhammas) convey the method, they are not to be clung to as though they were the experience. And of course, the experience is one of non-clinging.

To round off this chapter, here is a story told by the Buddha about mindfulness:

> At one time the Blessed One lived in the Sumbha country, near a town of the Sumbha people called Sedaka. There he addressed the monks as follows:
> 'In the past there was an acrobat who worked with a bamboo pole. Putting up his bamboo pole, he spoke to his girl apprentice Medakathalika, "Come, my dear, climb the pole and stand on my shoulders!" - "Yes, master" she said and did so. And the acrobat said: "Now, my dear, protect me well and I shall protect you. Thus watching over each other, protecting each other, we shall show our skill, make a living for ourselves, and get down safely from the bamboo pole."
> 'But Medakathalika the apprentice said: "Not so, master! You should protect yourself and I too shall protect myself. So self-guarded and self-protected we shall show our skill, earn our living, and get down safely from the bamboo pole."
> 'This is the right way' said the Blessed One and spoke further as follows:
> 'It is just as the apprentice said: "I shall protect myself," in that way the foundations of mindfulness should be practised. "I shall protect others," in that way they should be practised too. Protecting oneself one protects others; protecting others one protects oneself.
> 'And how does one in protecting oneself protect others? By patience and forbearance, by a non-violent and harmless life, by loving-kindness and compassion.
> '"I shall protect myself," in that way the foundations of mindfulness should be practised. "I shall protect others," in that way they should be practised too. Protecting oneself one protects others; protecting others one protects oneself'.[7]

Finally, there is this verse by the Buddha which again points out the Foundations of Mindfulness as the only way to Enlightenment:

> Having seen the end of birth,
> Compassionate for good, he knows
> the path that goes one way alone
> by which before they crossed as well,
> and in the future they will cross,
> and even now do cross the floods.[8]

NOTES TO CHAPTER III

[1] The best is: *The Heart of Buddhist Meditation* by Nyanaponika Thera (Rider & Co., London, and Samuel Weiser Inc., New York) This book has translations of the Buddha's Discourses on mindfulness with full explanations. See also the list of works issued by the Buddhist Publication Society, Kandy, Sri Lanka.

[2] *Sampajañña*, translated 'clear comprehension' by some authors.

[3] See *The Path of Purification*, trans. Nyanamoli Thera, Chapters XVII-XIX; *Dependent Origination*, Piyadassi Thera, Wheel 15 a/b; and *The Wheel of Birth and Death*, Bhikkhu Khantipalo, Wheel 147/149; all from B.P.S., Kandy.

[4] The Pali word *samma* can mean both intellectually right, and perfect in the sense of realization.

[5] *The Buddha's Ancient Path*, Piyadassi Mahathera, (B.P.S., Kandy), *The Life of the Buddha*, Bhikkhu Nyanamoli, (B.P.S., Kandy) and *The Word of the Buddha*, Nyanatiloka Mahathera, (B.P.S., Kandy). The last two books contain selected translations arranged to illustrate the Truths.

[6] See Note 4.

[7] Samvutta-nikaya (Related Discourses) XLVII.19. For notes on this Discourse see *The Heart of Buddhist Meditation* by Ven. Nyanaponika Mahathera.

[8] The four floods of sensuality, being (or existence), ignorance (of the Four Noble Truths) and Views. They are the same as the four taints (Chapter VIII).

And One's Heart well Purifying

IV

CALM AND INSIGHT

According to the Buddha's teachings meditation methods may either lead to calm or to insight, most meditation practice at the beginning, whether Buddhist or otherwise, being the development of calm. As most people develop this first and then, using it as a basis, experience insight, so we shall explain calm first and insight afterwards. However, a few may find that insight first and calm afterwards is the best path to follow, while many meditators use these differing approaches in an alternating way. Before the account of the development of calm it will be good to say something about balance of the faculties.

1. Balance of the Five Spiritual Faculties

These five - faith, effort, mindfulness, collectedness and wisdom - are often mentioned by the Buddha. When in harmonious balance they make for successful meditation but if some factors dominate while others are weak then growth will be one-sided and off-balance.

Faith and wisdom should be balanced. If faith is too strong while wisdom is weak then one will be credulous, believing anything or anyone and able to swallow the most fantastic ideas. This world has an abundance of such people! On the other hand, where wisdom is strong but faith weak, a person will be intellectual, possibly even cunning, and have little inclination towards practice. These two sorts of imbalance may be seen as people ruled either by their hearts (emotions) or their heads (intellect). They are illustrated in the Buddhist world by the pious traditional Buddhist who has little clear idea of why rituals are done or festivals held but just goes along with it anyway and gains emotional satisfaction from that; contrasted with the university educated person who has some Buddhist background but many more Buddhist books and can give long dissertations upon the Sarvastivadins and Sautrantikas (long-dead Buddhist sects) but never thinks of practising any Dhamma, even to the extent of a little giving, not to speak of meditation. From the point of view of training, the blind, faithful follower is to be preferred to the intellectual with a head full of ideas and a heart full of conceit. At least the former by practice can overcome blindness and come to understand Dhamma whereas the latter is unlikely ever to start practising.

Faith and wisdom should be balanced. What does this mean? Faith should be guided by wisdom; wisdom should be strengthened by faith. This can be illustrated with the story of the blind giant and the sharp-eyed cripple. The giant is strong and can travel great distances but he cannot see and so falls into pits and ditches; the cripple cannot walk but he has a pair of sharp eyes so he says to the giant, 'Hey, you put me up on your shoulders and I'll tell you the right way to go.' Then the pair of them travel far and wide and never take a wrong turning. When faith and wisdom are balanced, whatever is believed in is scrutinized by wisdom, while what is practised is strengthened by faith. One does not believe in wrong views in this way nor does one falter in practice of the right path.

Bhakti, the blind devotion to a guru or god, is not encouraged in the Buddha's Teachings. He did not want a lot of blind devotees who follow but who do not understand, the sort that may be compared to sheep. The Buddha's teachings are often known as 'lion's roars' because of their fearlessness and truthfulness. He encouraged those who were able to practise and to attain to be like lions, unafraid and direct. His training of Vakkali, a typical Indian bhakta or devotee illustrates this. Vakkali as a layman could never see enough of the Buddha's person so he decided to become a monk. After his ordination he followed the Buddha about everywhere watching the incomparable grace and mindfulness of the Master. Sometime later he fell ill and, since he could no longer see the Buddha, became depressed. The monks attending him asked why he was sad and he told them. They invited the Buddha to come and console Vakkali. When the Master arrived, after making Vakkali admit why he was sad, he said to him 'Vakkali, what is there in seeing this vile body! He who sees Dhamma sees me; he who sees me sees Dhamma.' After this strong medicine Vakkali's health improved and he was able to attain Enlightenment as an Arahant.

Effort and collectedness should also be balanced. With too much effort and too little collectedness there is distraction or restlessness, while an imbalance the other way leads to lethargy and possibly to trance states where there is no mindfulness. Too great an effort has already been illustrated with the case of Venerable Sona Thera (Chapter II.2) but usually people make too little effort. They do not make effort with the unwholesome and wholesome states of mind in everyday life as described in Chapter Two, so how will they make effort with sitting and walking meditation? If one sits for only ten minutes when really one has time to sit thirty minutes, this is because of lack of effort. And without it one's practice never seems to get anywhere so one becomes disheartened, gives it up and slides back into some old rut. More dukkha!

Mindfulness, the middle faculty in the list of five, is like the upright of a balance - the pans may be out of balance but the upright stays where it is. This faculty is basic to the growth of the other four. While they can be too strongly developed this never applies to mindfulness which should be allowed to grow and strengthen to the highest degree.

Neither calm nor insight succeed unless they are based on the balance of faculties, so if one meditates one should consider which are well developed and which have to be strengthened and then take the appropriate steps. Faith is strengthened by going to see Teachers, listening to their Dhamma and by efforts to practise what they teach. Devotional practice in a shrineroom also strengthens faith.[1] Effort is strengthened through determination and by actually doing meditation regularly. One should attempt something which is a little difficult - getting up earlier for instance, and keep it up! Collectedness is strengthened by increased daily mindfulness with more effort. The mindfulness prevents drifting into trance states, about which more will be said below. Wisdom is strengthened by persistent effort to be mindful of defilements, as well as by using methods to combat them. And mindfulness strengthens them all.

2. The Development of Calm

In the beginning of Chapter Two the usual condition of the mind has been analysed. If we are dissatisfied with it and take up meditation what sort of things may happen and what special obstacles are there to the attainment of deep concentration? The first part of the question is better answered in Chapter Six while here we shall be concerned first with the Five Hindrances and then with the different states of samadhi or deep concentration (or *jhāna*).

The five hindrances are usually mentioned by the Buddha before his description of the four jhanas. If one's meditation does not succeed then it is because of the presence of one or more of them. They may be compared not so much to barriers across a road as to high hedges and banks along its sides which prevent one from gaining a wide view. Another way of picturing them is as a 'layer' of the defilements. They are not so coarse as the defilements which bring about the breaking of the Five Precepts but they are not so fine as the three or four Taints (Chapter VIII). Their relation to the three Unwholesome Roots is easy to see:-

Roots:	Greed	Aversion	Delusion
Hindrances:	Sensual Desire	Ill-Will	Lethargy and Drowsiness
			Agitation and Worry
			Sceptical Doubt

No less than three of them arise from delusion - this indicates that persistent effort will be needed to overcome the hindrances as the root of delusion is harder to see than those of greed and aversion.

The hindrance of sensual desire can be seen when a meditator starts thinking thoughts connected with various pleasures - just the way to destroy any calm he may have had! Sometimes a certain anxiety arises because the mind is too still and the ego or self starts to throw up memories or ideas of pleasure so as to increase the flow of mental stimulation. The pleasures remembered may be coarse or subtle but they have the same result - loss of concentration. The Buddha compared this hindrance to water in a jar to which colours have been added. Then a person looking into the water would not be able to see his face, in the same way the meditator is not able to see his 'own face', the pure mind.

This hindrance, because it is connected with pleasant things, is not easy to give up. The Commentaries suggest the following

Calm and Insight

methods for doing so:-
   (i) Paying attention to and meditating upon the unattractive side of life. (Contemplation of the Unattractive in Chapter V.).
   (ii) Guarding the doors of the senses.
   (iii) Moderation in eating (See Chapter I.5).
   (iv) Friendship with Noble Persons, which means having a meditation Teacher and going to see him frequently.
   (v) Talk about Dhamma and not about worldly things.

Ill-will is a hindrance which destroys calm even faster than sensual desire. Thoughts of enmity, resentment, rejection or revenge instantly shatter whatever peace has been developed. They may be directed at particular people, or at situations one dislikes, or more abstractly at institutions and places. None of such thoughts can be justified in terms of 'righteous' because Buddhist psychology does not recognize that any kind of anger can be right or good. Anger, hatred and ill-will, all of them spring up from the unwholesome root of aversion, are therefore unwholesome themselves and lead to an unwholesome fruit, a result which will be painful and undesired. The Buddha has compared the mind of ill-will to a pot of water heated over a fire, boiling and seething - and again a man could not recognize his own face reflected in it. Modern Buddhist tradition too in Thailand speaks of people who are impatient, hurried, rough and angry as 'hot-hearted', they are on fire inside with this hindrance.

Helpful in ridding oneself of this hindrance are the following practices:
   (i) The practice of Loving-kindness (see next chapter).
   (ii) Frequently considering: 'I am the owner of my kamma, heir to my kamma, born of my kamma, related to my kamma, abide supported by my kamma; whatever kamma I shall do, whether good or evil, of that I shall be the heir.' (The Buddha's words).
   (iii) Frequent reflection on the evils and dangers springing from ill-will.
   (iv) Friendship with Noble people.
   (v) Suitable conversation, especially avoiding that which criticizes or disparages others, or will be harmful to them in some way.

The third hindrance, lethargy and drowsiness, can be seen among meditators when their heads begin to nod and it can be heard among them when their breathing becomes deep even if they do not actually snore! But it begins before these outward signs are clear, the mind starts to go fuzzy and out of focus. It shrinks and will not stretch over one's meditation subject. Here are some of the Buddha's recommendations for curing it, methods he taught Venerable Maha-Moggallāna, his chief left-hand disciple, before the latter's attainment of Arahantship.
   (i) Know the thoughts that give rise to this hindrance and give them no attention.
   (ii) Reflect on the Dhamma which one has heard.
   (iii) Learn by heart (chant) something from the Dhamma.
   (iv) Pull one's ears and rub one's limbs. (The earlobes when pulled hard dispel drowsiness).

(v) Get up, wash the face, gaze around especially at the starry sky.

(vi) Visualize in one's mind a great light like the sun at midday.

(vii) Do walking-meditation with the mind turned inwards not to outer things.

(viii) Finally, if none of these work then lie down mindfully on the right side in the lion-posture, mindfully aware of the time to get up. When one wakes, get up immediately and do not indulge in further sleep.

Also helpful for curing this hindrance are the recollections of death, of the dukkha inherent in impermanent and conditioned things, and stimulation of the mind by arousing interest, rapture and bliss. A meditation which does this, the Recollection of the Buddha, will be described in the next chapter.

The Buddha's simile for this hindrance is a jar of water overgrown with slime and water-plants, the thick covering of which make it impossible for a man to see his own face. The 'sliminess' of this hindrance emphasizes the difficulty of ridding the mind of it especially in the small hours of the morning!

Agitation and Worry, the fourth hindrance, is also well-known to meditators. 'My mind doesn't keep still for even a second' or 'I lost the meditation subject after the first five minutes' - these are common reports by meditation beginners. And many people are amazed at how restless 'their own mind' is when they first sit down to practise. The Buddha compared the untrained mind to a wild bull elephant which has been accustomed to going where it pleased. After a while it is captured and its feet tied by leather thongs to a great post. Then it bucks and stamps and kicks. The mind is like this too and may actually seem to be wilder than usual when meditation practice is begun but this may be only that one has more mindfulness and so notices mental wanderings more easily.

This is a hindrance for which the cure is rather the whole of the Buddha's Dhamma (Teaching) and Vinaya (Discipline - the Five Precepts for instance). Steadiness in one's practice is helpful, that is, doing it at the same time and for the same length of time every day. It also helps if one does not travel anywhere. The mind which is very ready to travel even if the body is sitting still can have a fine distracting time when the body moves too. Staying for as long as one can with a good Teacher in a quiet secluded place is the best cure for this sickness but even then the mind can find something to do.

The mind's constant movement when afflicted with this hindrance is illustrated in the simile of a full water-pot over which the wind is blowing so that ripples are formed all the time. One cannot see one's own face clearly then.

The last of the hindrances is sceptical doubt or uncertainty. This is not doubt that is easily cured by asking a question: this is rather doubting what should be done or what should be followed. Intelligent people are often afflicted with this hindrance - they doubt what is quite clear to others, they do not see which course of action to take or else they are uncertain about very straightforward teachings. Due to this they find it hard even to begin practising Dhamma. If they do so, then a host of questions may arise in their minds which no answers will satisfy. They are all the time swaying on top of the uncomfortable wall on which they sit but never get their feet down on the ground on either side. The doubt and uncertainty which they experience is often of the sort which compares (say) the teachings of Jesus with the Buddha's but is unable to decide what should be done. A great deal of time can be wasted in this way.

The sort of thoughts which can arise to disturb a meditator are 'Maybe the Buddha wasn't really enlightened' or 'Perhaps my Teacher doesn't know either - he just gets it all from a book' or 'I ought to go now and practise with...' (some other Teacher or Teaching).

Obviously the best cure for doubt is thorough learning guided by a good Teacher from whom one may ask all the questions. On the basis of that learning and those questions one can acquire strong confidence in the Buddha, Dhamma and Sangha. Devotional practices are also useful, such as taking offerings to a temple or shrineroom, prostration and chanting the Buddha's discourses.

The deluded nature of this hindrance may be appreciated from the simile for it: A pot full of muddy water which has been stirred up is put away in a dark place. Even in muddy water one's face is not easily seen, let alone when it is kept in darkness!

The usual mental states which are called five-door consciousness together with the reflection upon the input received, tie one to the kama-world, the states of existence based on sensual experience. As we have pointed out, sensuality is forever tied up with dukkha so the meditator recognizing this tries to transcend the five-door consciousness and the discursive thought-filled mind. When the five hindrances all disappear another type of mind will be known which does not depend on continual stimulation for happiness. The experience of rapture and bliss arises due to its purity and concentration. It does not wander. It has one subject continually. And its emotional content is not the desire/aversion basis of sensual experience but loving-kindness and compassion for all beings.

The sort of mind which has been described in brief above is called jhana (from a root meaning 'burning-up' - of defilements) and it gives access to other planes of existence called the Brahma-world, the refined heavens of subtle form. This is not the place to say much about them and even the Buddha has left hardly any descriptions of them. No doubt the trouble is that words are inadequate for this purpose. Even his descriptions of jhana are brief and limited to a list of psychological factors, illuminated on a few occasions by similes which we shall give below.

Before coming to the jhanas a word should be said on two things: trances and 'neighbourhood' concentration.

Some authors have translated jhana with 'trance' but this is very misleading as the experience of these two is quite distinct. Trance is a state near to sleep, where mindfulness is very weak and the mind rather dull. People who sit in 'meditation', sometimes for hours, but on being asked 'Where was your mind? What were you aware of?' reply 'Oh, just grey blankness. I wasn't aware of anything', - have been in a trance. Obviously the third hindrance has been turned full on! There is no advantage in being able to sit long in a trance. If this becomes habitual it may become difficult to avoid sliding into one, so mindfulness should check the mind constantly as the meditation proceeds to see that it does not happen. Typical symptoms after emergence from a trance are heaviness of body and dullness of mind, the eyes feel glued up and one feels like more sleep straight away! Trances should also be avoided because of the tendency some people have to get in contact with other beings who can, while they are in trance, temporarily take over. The aim of Dhamma has nothing to do with mediumship or messages 'from the other side'. One should remember that the beings sending such messages, if beings they are and not the medium's subconscious, are also deluded. They are not enlightened! But their messages are able to convince credulous people easily. More will be said on possession in Chapter Seven.

Neighbourhood concentration is experience of a state of tranquillity near to jhana. It sometimes happens that a meditator has the experience of an instant of profound peace, a fraction of a second when the mind goes down into the heart. The usual startled reaction is to think 'What was that!' This instant is a momentary experience of neighbourhood concentration or it could even be a jhana. As the practice deepens such flashes may lengthen in time and become more familiar, so that anxiety is not aroused. And it does appear at those times that one's 'centre' is no longer up in the head where all the senses are but deep in one's heart.

The experience is not necessarily peaceful in that visions may arise at this time. They may be very pleasant and delightful ones - of the devas for instance and their heavenly worlds, or fearful ones - of one's own body decaying. In the first case the danger is that one becomes fascinated with the new worlds which have opened up, their colours and forms and their inhabitants - there is no end to this distraction. Some who experience only this are quite content to play around with these images and do not realize that they are trapped by their own clinging and cannot make any further progress. The fearful visions, of decay, disease and death, can have worse results for timid minds. Such people have been known to go mad after seeing these things. The importance of a good Teacher to direct one's meditation is again clear.

Neighbourhood concentration is like unexplored country, it is not the familiar world of five-door consciousness and the mental reflections on this. What will be found in this unknown region depends largely on what sort of kamma one has made. Some people's experience of it is extensive and their minds like to explore this area. Others do not have the kammic tendencies which keep them to this concentration and proceed straight to jhana which is also known as full concentration.

The Commentaries in explaining these states have rather stylized human psychology. Visions and what they signify are classified too rigidly. By contrast, people have a great variety of experiences which do not fit these traditional categories very well. For this reason they have not been given here. The Commentaries do rightly emphasize that in the jhanas there is no experinece of sensual consciousness. A person in jhana does not see, hear, smell, taste or touch anything – their 'five-door' consciousness is stilled. But their mind-door consciousness is super-concentrated and bright, so that jhana cannot be mistaken for a hypnotic or cataleptic trance.

When jhana occurred to the Buddha-to-be for the first time his description of his mental state emphasizes what we shall need if we are to do the same. 'Tireless energy was aroused in me and unforgetting mindfulness established, my body was tranquil and untroubled, my mind was concentrated and unified.'[2] The Buddha's usual description of the first jhana which is repeated many times in his discourses, follows. In it, the words 'unwholesome dhammas' refer to the five hindrances. 'Quite secluded from sensual desires, secluded from unwholesome dhammas, I entered upon and abode in the first jhana which is accompanied by *initial and sustained application*, with *rapture* and *bliss* born of seclusion.'

Now some explanation should be given to the four factors in italics above, plus the fifth one which is *one-pointedness of mind*, as the English is lacking words defining the subtleties of meditation.

Initial application (*vitakka*) means the fine constant effort to keep the mind pointed at the meditation subject. This effort must not be too strong otherwise the subtle balance of mind will be disturbed. It is compared to the repeated soft notes struck on a gong. Although in other contexts *vitakka* can mean 'thinking' it is misleading to translate it in the jhana-formula in this way. 'Thinking', the stream of words and pictures we usually call mind, is quietened long before jhana is experienced. A meditator can have a wordless and concentrated mind but not be in jhana yet, so the translation 'initial application' is much to be preferred.

The next factor, sustained application, (*vicāra*) follows on from the first. It is the sustained direction of mind when concentration is complete. The Commentaries compare it to the reverberations of the gong which continue for some time after it has been struck. It could be compared to the impetus that a model car has when pushed over a smooth surface, the initial push being the previous factor. 'Sustained application' has also the sense of exploration or continued examination though we should remember that this is done without words. It is certainly very wrong to translate this 'discursive thinking', as some authors have done.

Pīti or 'rapture' is another word which defies translation. Its nature is most easily understood from its physical manifestations, though in jhana these are very refined. In ordinary mental states it is quite common to experience something of rapture especially the first kind – 'minor rapture', defined as able to raise the hairs on the body. 'Momentary rapture' is compared to lightning flashes in different parts of the body and lasting only a brief time. But with 'overflowing rapture' there is a repeated swell or flow so that the body feels as though waves were breaking again and again. The fourth variety 'uplifting rapture' can actually cause the body to lift off the ground. The body of one who experiences this rapture feels like a feather and has lost the earthy weightiness usually asociated with the physical body. It can indeed float or fly but this is merely a by-product of meditation development and should not sidetrack efforts to attain jhana. The last aspect of rapture is call 'pervading' as when a great mountain cave is suddenly filled with a hugh flood of water. This is the aspect of rapture found in the first jhana. Though rapture has been illustrated by what it does to the body yet it is a mental factor and one which continues on from sustained application, for its gradual strengthening means that interest becomes stronger and the direction of the mind has greater impetus towards one-pointedness. More will be said upon rapture in Chapter Six.

Bliss (*sukha*) is more refined than rapture and definitely an extension, in a subtle way, of happy feeling. But this happiness is so fine due to the purity of mind that it cannot be imagined by those who have not meditated. It furthers concentration and because of its wonderful blissfulness leads the meditator to continue efforts to one-pointedness.

This last factor, (*ekaggatā*) is the bringing of all the mind's power together, the complete focusing of the mind to only one point, the meditation subject which is constantly the mind's object. (Here though, it is difficult to talk of subject and object, for the mind in jhana becomes the subject - Loving-kindness, Mindfulness with Breathing or whatever has been used to develop meditation). The mind however, does need such one-pointed attention otherwise no meditation will be developed, let alone a jhana experience.

These five factors found in the first jhana can of course be experienced by a meditator long before jhana. But in that case they are isolated from each other or not in balance. They have to be carefully cultivated and harmonized so that one leads on to the production of the next until when they are complete, jhana is experienced.

It is worth noting here, as elsewhere, the Buddha has shown how factors give rise to other factors through repeated practice, and the culmination of this process, here jhana, is the natural result of this. Jhana in Buddhism is never looked on as 'a gift' or as 'supernatural', it just happens to those who patiently cultivate. And though it is so different from ordinary five-door consciousness which does not operate at all in jhana, it is not something from outside oneself, only a subtle exploration of the purified heights of which 'mind' is capable of knowing. This is emphasized by the simile which the Buddha gives for this jhana:

> Just as a skilled bathman or his apprentice heaps bath-powder in a metal basin, and sprinkling it gradually with water, kneads it up till the moisture wets his ball of bath-powder, soaks it, and extends over it within and without though the ball itself does not become liquid, so too the bhikkhu makes rapture born of seclusion drench, steep, fill and extend throughout this body so that there is nothing of his whole body to which it does not extend.

The importance given to rapture and its suffusion throughout the body should be noted. As it is a conditionally produced dhamma, however, it cannot be forced to occur. All the other factors of

Calm and Insight

Dhamma-practice which make for it must be present – among them, purity of virtue and effort are the most important.

Progress to the second jhana means relinquishing those factors which are grossest in the first. Initial and sustained application which are essential for the latter must be calmed down for the second jhana to occur. Here is the Buddha's description of it: 'With the stilling of initial and sustained application he enters upon and abides in the second jhana, which has inner tranquillity and onepointedness of mind, without initial and sustained application, with rapture and bliss born of concentration.'

In the second jhana where rapture and bliss are born of concentration they are more subtle than in the first where they arise from the seclusion of the mind which has no hindrances. It is illustrated with the following simile:

> Just as if there were a lake whose waters welled up from below, having no inflow from east, west, north or south, nor yet replenished from time to time with showers from the skies, then the cool fount of water welling up in the lake would make the cool water drench, steep, fill and extend throughout the lake, and there would be nothing of the whole lake to which the cool water did not extend; so too the bhikkhu makes rapture and bliss born of concentration drench, steep, fill and extend through the body, so that there is nothing of his whole body to which they do not extend.

Note should be taken that in the second jhana both rapture and bliss pervade the whole body, and that they are described as welling up from below. More will be said about this in Chapter Six.

In the third jhana the description and simile run like this:

> With the fading as well of rapture he abides in equanimity, mindful and fully aware, still feeling bliss with the body, he enters upon and abides in the third jhana, on which account Noble Ones announce 'He has a blissful abiding who has equanimity and is mindful'. Just as, in a pond of blue, white or red lotuses, some are born under the water, grow under water and do not emerge from it but flourish immersed in it, and the water drenches, steeps, fills and extends throughout them to their tips and roots and there is nothing of the whole of those lotuses to which it does not extend; so too the bhikkhu makes the bliss divested of rapture drench, steep, fill and extend throughout this body till there is nothing of his whole body to which it does not extend.

As rapture is relinquished this jhana is more subtle than the second though bliss is still experienced. Many meditators cannot pass beyond second or third jhanas because they become attached to the grosser rapture or the finer bliss. These things are difficult to put down especially when they are accompanied by views and visions which will be discussed below. This is a 'blissful abiding', a meditation state of purified happiness where one may stay for longer or shorter periods of time according to one's development. The water which in the first jhana simile pervaded the ball of powder and in the second welled up from below, now covers the meditator completely. He is submerged in bliss.

When one is willing to relinquish even this bliss then the fourth jhana follows:

> With the abandoning of pleasure (*sukha*) and pain (*dukkha*), and with the previous disappearance of joy and grief, he enters upon and abides in the fourth jhana which has neither-pain-nor-pleasure and has purity of mindfulness due to equanimity. Just as if a man were sitting clothed from head to foot in white cloth, and there was nothing of his whole body to which the white cloth did not extend, so too the bhikkhu sits with pure bright cognizance extending over his body and there is nothing of his whole body to which it does not extend.

The emphasis has changed here with the relinquishing of rapture and bliss. Their importance is stressed with the water similes but here the factors emphasized are 'purity of mindfulness due to equanimity', so a 'drier' simile evoking purity, that of white cloth, is used by the Buddha.

This purity is also known as 'liberation of the heart' because one who attains it and continues to practise it manifests to others no more greed and aversion and has only subtle attachments to existence on the jhana levels, that is the worlds of subtle form or Brahma-worlds, or to the formless worlds. Others meeting such a person would rightly hold him to be a saint but they would be wrong if they took him to be completely liberated, though the heart is liberated of unwholesome desires while practice continues yet the mind as a whole can still harbour wrong views. The Arahant, by contrast is often spoken of as one who has experienced both liberation of the heart *and* liberation by wisdom.

Before we pursue this line of thought, the formless concentrations may be mentioned. They are attainable on the basis of the fourth jhana and are described only by their names:

Infinity of space,
Infinity of consciousness,
No-thingness,
Neither-perception-nor-non-perception.

No words were used by the Buddha to elaborate upon them, presumably because they are so far beyond the range of words. Some meditators from all religions having mystical traditions experience them, and as with the four jhanas, may be misled by their interpretation of them. However, the Buddha encourages one to see them as conditioned states and not as the ultimate goal. Meditators who lack good advice might take, for instance, the infinity of space experience to be voidness (see Chapter VIII) and imagine therefore that they had arrived at the ultimate truth of not-self. But this is to confuse an experience of calm with an insight experience; in the former though there is mindfulness present there is no penetrative

Calm and Insight

wisdom and actually no defilements are cut off. Those who take any of these eight attainments to be the goal and have the death-consciousness fully concentrated on these planes just continue to exist there when the human body dies. What such existence, with no body at all and a mind centred on, say, infinite space, could be like can only be known to those who have had the experience of the concentration of infinite space. It is not possible to develop insight on the basis of these formless concentrations but if a meditator has great ability he can work his way through all of them and then arrive at cessation-attainment in which there is no perception or feeling. Emerging from that, insight development is possible and in fact the Paths and Fruits may be experienced. But this is the way only for those who are very strong in calm and so applies only to a few of those who reach Noble attainments.

Teachers in north-east Thailand usually do not identify any of these attainments when asked by a pupil about some meditation experience. Obviously the danger is that the pupil will get stuck with ideas of 'I have attained first jhana!' - or whatever. They may be identified by those who experience them if they wish but the name of the experience is not as important as the use to which it is put.

Emergence from any of the jhanas should be gentle and gradual. The meditator should not move suddenly. It is advisable that if a person has to be aroused from deep meditation states, something which should only be done if really necessary, a small bell or gong be rung very softly until he or she begins to move. It is important that the meditator should not be shocked out of jhana by any rough or violent action.

When a person emerges from jhana the first time his view of what has happened will depend to some extent on what he has been conditioned to believe. The jhana-experience is so different from the usual states of wholesome and unwholesome 'minds' that a meditator with a theistic background could easily identify the bliss, rapture, and sense of oneness with God, or as his true Self or Soul. Ordinarily he knows his own mind as varying between wholesome, unwholesome and neutral states - that is what he identifies as being 'himself', so then if he should experience totally purified consciousness it is easy to label that 'not self but the gift of another' and then fit the experience into the terms of a theology already held to be true.

A Buddhist is careful not to do this. He knows that whatever arises, bliss, rapture, 'oneness' or visions - does so because of supporting conditions, continues while those conditions give support and passes away with the changing of those conditions. This applies to everything contained in the five aggregates which is the totality of oneself. He knows too that mind-heart is capable of a much wider range of experience than that perceived through the five sense-doors with mind as the sixth. All that is experienced should be tested to find out 'Does it arise conditionally?' If it does then it will pass away too and so cannot be grasped at as Ultimate Reality under any such names as God, Soul, Self, Godhead, Cosmic Consciousness and so on.

People who do not practise meditation usually have much

attachment to sensual pleasures but meditators, especially those who experience jhana, can become deeply attached to rapture and bliss even though they have few worldly attachments. When this is the case no further progress is possible so meditators are encouraged by the Buddha to reflect upon the conditioned nature of their blissful experience, to see it as *impermanent* and therefore as subject to deterioration. Whatever has this characteristic is also unreliable and insecure, which is the most subtle aspect of *dukkha*. Then again experience which is liable to deteriorate and change, to be unsatisfactory, can scarcely be my *self* (or Soul). In this way the Three Characteristics can be used to break up attachment to even subtle meditation states.

3. Preliminary Considerations to Insight

Enlightenment (*bodhi*) cannot be reached by calm alone. By way of the development of calm the hindrances can be overcome - while practice continues, the jhanas enjoyed and the heart's liberation experienced. Still some aspects of the mind are not purified and some layers of defilements not yet cut off.

This may be illustrated by the stories of the well-known teachers of meditation just prior to the Buddha's days, Alara Kalama and Uddaka Ramaputta. Before his enlightenment while he was still an ascetic wandering in search of the truth, Gotama went to see these teachers and became their disciple. He mastered their teachings and then practised meditation up to the same levels as those teachers themselves had attained. The first of them had experienced the formless base consisting of No-thingness, while the second had known Neither-perception-nor-non-perception. When he had also won these attainments, though those teachers offered him the place of co-teacher and sole teacher over their groups of disciples yet Gotama reflected in this way: 'This Dhamma does not lead to dispassion, to the fading of lust, to cessation, to peace, to direct-knowledge, to enlightenment, to Nibbana, but only to the base consisting of no-thingness (or to neither-perception...) I was not satisfied with that Dhamma. I left it to pursue my search.'

What the exact teachings of these two were is not recorded, only that they led to the highest of the formless states. They were truly masters of meditation but Gotama the wanderer was not satisfied with what they taught. No doubt he found that while he practised meditation the defilements nearly vanished but could always reappear if meditation ceased. Moreover, he was not satisfied with the conditioned nature of those formless attainments even though they were very pure and exalted. He saw in their conditionedness the possibility of deterioration, of unsatisfactoriness and that even with them a subtle sense of self existed and that self-identification was not cut off through them. He saw that by themselves they were not a way out.

If for a moment we leave consideration of these exalted states and that long ago time and look at our own days there is something useful to learn from the comparison. Then as now many teachers

Calm and Insight 63.

taught meditation and no doubt some of them in those times used mantras. Now we find the repetition of mantras very popular among both Buddhists and non-Buddhists and it is said that this kind of practice alone will bring liberation or salvation. When we consider what mantra-repetition involves it is clear that it will develop calm, including jhanas and formless states, but how in this way can insight be developed? Practice with a mantra does not develop the perceptions of impermanence, dukkha and not-self so that liberation by wisdom, the fruit of complete enlightenment cannot be won with it. This applies whatever mantra is considered, whether Hail Marys, the Jesus Prayer or Hare Krishna... In the southern Buddhist countries too a repetition word is sometimes used like 'Buddho', 'Sammā Arahaṁ' or 'Namo vimuttāmaṁ namo vimuttiyā'[3]. But by these words alone one does not reach enlightenment. In Burma it is a widespread practice to recite using a rosary 'Anicca Dukkha Anattā'[4] but even in this case if the words are used mantra-fashion to calm down the mind they will not lead to insight into those Three Characteristics.

Perhaps a brief digression would be useful here to consider why there is no trace of mantra-repetition in the Buddha's original teaching that we find in the Pali Canon. In the Buddha's days the people who taught mantras were the brahmins and the mantras they imparted were the Vedas themselves and other material based on them. 'Manta' the Pali form of mantra actually often has the meaning of 'Vedic Hymn'. Now some of these 'hymns' specially those of the Atharva, the fourth Veda, are really spells designed to bring about one's desired objectives, whether they are wholesome or not. There are mantras for opening locks (handy for thieves!) and others for obtaining the love of a woman (whether already married or not). Such a belief in the magical power of certain words cuts right across the Buddha's Teaching of 'Every evil never doing, and in wholesomeness increasing, and one's heart well-purifying - This is the Buddhas' Teaching'. The latter is the way out of superstition and of all the blameable fraud connected with magic, omens and signs and the rest. This was the brahmins' sphere and the Buddha left it to them! But when asked questions upon such matters the Buddha criticized brahminical pretensions and superstition. There is the nicely ironical story told by the Buddha of the brahmin who had a set of fine clothes gnawed by rats and in deadly fear of bad luck had them cast in the charnel ground. The Buddha went there and picked them up to make a set of robes at which the brahmin hurried to warn him of his danger. Then the Buddha had a chance to teach him what was truly auspicious.

Later Buddhists, influenced by the prevailing religious trends in India, incorporated thousands of mantras into Buddhist works, often one suspects with the motive of having more powerful spells than the Hindu (or Jain) outfit next door! However, in the Buddha's original teachings there is no trace of the doctrine that particular sounds in the mantra have particular effects, or that they will affect particular parts of the body. All this comes from brahminical influence and is far from Buddha's way of insight. So a mantra, even a Buddhist one, cannot lead by its repetition to insight and enlightenment, only to calm.

Above we quoted again the verse called 'The Heart of the Buddhas' Teachings' which covers the full extent of what Gotama the Buddha taught. Thus:
'Every evil never doing' = virtue, the Five (etc.) Precepts,
'and in wholesomeness increasing' = meditation (calm),
'and one's heart well-purifying' = wisdom (insight).

Virtue, as we have seen, means purity of all body and speech actions. Then meditation, meaning here the development of calm, purifies the mind - for instance, of the five hindrances. So what does wisdom, or the insight meditation by which it is developed, purify?

Insight-wisdom purifies views. It is very important to understand what is meant by a 'view'. By this word are covered assumptions, opinions, beliefs and speculations. Let us look at these a little closer. I assume upon waking each morning that the body lying in bed is my body, belongs to me, I am lying there - this is an assumption automatically made without any reflection. I may also have certain opinions about this body - that this kind of food is good for it and that not good, ideas which arise after a certain amount of reflection. And I may hold beliefs about this body - that it may be resurrected in future for instance. Such beliefs imply a faith-commitment to some religious teaching and may or may not involve reflection according to whether one tends to accept doctrines, or philosophize about them. Speculations are the result of thinking about, elaborating upon and filling in the philosophic chinks in a system. And system-making involves all the other three shades of view, especially assumptions. When a person assumes something which is not really true it is possible through others' teaching and his own experience for him to see at first intellectually, his mistaken assumption. But if he has opinions on the matter - food or politics maybe, it will be harder for him to see what is not true in them. If beliefs are involved, meaning the teachings peculiar to certain religions, then it will be very difficult for him to see things clearly, while if the beliefs have been elaborated into a philosophy there is not much hope that he can ever see things in a way differing from his system.

We cling to views. They make up one leg upon which the concept of self-soul rests, the other two being craving and conceit (or conceptualizing). Views support the self-concept, they are the very root of it, for the basic concept is 'I am' - upon which all views are founded. They all involve various tenses of the verb 'to be': I was, I shall be, I am - and the negative forms I was not, I shall not be, I am not. Out of this basic material is formed the countless thousands of views which people hold. As views are so near the self-concept it is not surprising that they are clung to, even defended fiercely. They have been in the past and are now too the cause for much dukkha, even for murder and massacre. There is nothing that fanatics - those who get great self-satisfaction and reassurance from their rigid views, will not do in the name of what they blindly hold to be true.

Clinging (upādāna) in any way is a spiritual obstacle. It is true that some clinging, to sensual pleasures for instance, is a grosser

Calm and Insight

obstacle than other sorts. And clinging to a religious view may not obstruct the attainment of the jhanas in this life and the Brahma-world heavens in the next, provided that there is a firm basis of virtue. But clinging to views does obstruct the attainment of enlightenment, for this is characterized by non-clinging, no clinging to anything - body, feeling, perception, mental formations and consciousness. Holding views entails strong clinging to mental formations backed up by feeling.

What kinds of views are there? They may be divided into Wrong Views with fixed destiny, Wrong Views with no fixed destiny, Mundane Right View and Supermundane Right (Perfect) View. And the last one can also be called No View.

'Wrong View with fixed destiny' means the sort of entrenched views which lead people holding them to do evil, to break the precepts, to make unwholesome kamma. As an example Communist fanatics may be cited; they believe that by killing off a certain part of the population a better and more equitable society will come about. In this case, the doctrine itself incites to violence and class-hatred - so since this is just aversion, the second root of unwholesomeness, one may expect followers to express their hatred (and envy) in acts of speech and body. Having killed the class-enemies, though they believe they have acted rightly, they will quickly reap a 'fixed destiny' in the next birth, a painful one which will continue for very long. The twisted and thuggish people who ran Hitler's extermination camps had similar wrong views concerning the Jews. And twisted individuals too who inflict suffering on their families with the belief that it is good for those who suffer - they too have wrong view with fixed destiny, though probably to a lesser degree. Religious fanatics in the past could also be found who believed that the persecutions they organized had Divine Sanction, while it is still possible to find 'religiously-inspired' soldiers who fight and kill with the belief that their actions will lead them to Heaven. In general, this kind of wrong view, the worst and most blameable in terms of the sufferings caused, is rooted in aversion and leads to violence and harshness.

By contrast, in 'Wrong Views with no fixed destiny', the roots of greed and delusion are more prominent. We are deluded and have wrong views about the five aggregates when we consider 'these are mine, I am these, these are my self (soul)'. But from holding such a view which is deeply embedded there is no certain result for one may, holding this view, nevertheless make much good kamma. This is a wrong view - for analysis reveals no 'I', 'self' or 'owner', but it is unformulated. A formulated wrong view of this sort means the holding as true such doctrines as the Trinity in Christianity, or the one indivisible God in Islam, or a multiplicity of gods which are all reflections of a Divine ground for existence as in the Advaita Vedanta of Hinduism. Here are three very different beliefs, each of which is held to be true by its followers. It is characteristic of views even when they do not give rise to violence, always to produce division and contention. The material found in views, the doctrines which are believed, also have the characteristic of being unprovable and in the last resort when logic has failed, just have to be believed or rejected. Wrong views of this sort which are formulated into doctrines may not lead their followers to make any unwholesome kamma by body or speech, in fact of course they may be excellent people making much good kamma by giving, virtue and the development of calm meditation. In this way there is no 'fixed and painful result' for them but rather much future happiness. But wrong view with no fixed destiny does obstruct the cultivation of wisdom and will ensure that insight meditation (*vipassanā-bhāvanā*) even if practised will give no liberating result. Clinging to views obstructs liberation.

An example will illustrate this. A Roman Catholic monk practises zazen (sitting in meditation) in a Zen monastery in Kyoto. Going for interview one day his Teacher tells him: 'You have to give up God!' (That is, he has to give up attachment to his concept 'God' and let go of it completely). What is he to do? If he gives up God he can develop insight (*vipassanā*) but he must cease to be a Catholic. If he does not then he stays inside the Church but can get no further with his practice. His meditations on calm may be very fine but insight-wisdom cannot develop due to his clinging to views.

The Buddha defined Right View as the Four Noble Truths. Mundane Right View is having a clear understanding of the principles of those Truths, that is, by study and intellectual thought. Why did he make these Noble Truths the focus of his teaching? Why are they called Right View? The Buddha is like a doctor who visits a sick person. The doctor examines the patient to discover the symptoms, then from his knowledge he diagnoses the cause. Having done so he prescribes medicines to be taken regularly and he says to the sufferer 'If you take this medicine as prescribed you should be well after some time'. The Buddha as the Physician of the World sees the troubles people suffer – dukkha both gross and subtle. His diagnosis is that this arises from the various sorts of craving. More craving = more dukkha. He prescribed the medicines of virtue, meditation and insight-wisdom and expects, if these are applied as he instructs, that a complete cure will result. The difference between the doctors of this world and the Teacher of doctors is that the former cure only the body, their 'cures' of the mind touching only the symptoms, not the causes, besides which their patients can fall ill again; whereas the Buddha treats the mind directly out of which come many ills, bodily as well as mental, and the cure he offers, if the complete course of his medicine is taken, is irreversible. The disease of dukkha is cured forever.

If one looks at one's own life it can be seen very clearly as a search for happiness and satisfaction. How hard one tries to avoid suffering and pain! For this reason the Four Noble Truths of Dukkha, Causal Arising, Cessation and Path are central both to knowledge about and penetration into the Dhamma. They are correctly called Right View!

Supermundane Right View, which may also be called Perfect View, means just this penetration in oneself of the Truths. And this implies the giving up of craving and clinging, even to the view of self,

Calm and Insight

so that there is no more attachment to any sort of views. A Buddhist can easily be attached to the Dhamma. He then has mundane Right View. By practice of Dhamma, including meditation, he gives up that clinging and having seen the Dhamma or Truth, there exists just supermundane Right View, or no view at all. This should be called 'holding no view', just as the Buddha held no view. He characterized holding views as 'the thicket of views, the wilderness of views, the contortion of views, the vacillation of views, the fetter of views.' There is no end to the jungle of views unless there is Right View.

The Buddha spoke of the two aspects of Right View in a simile; Suppose a person stands on the bank of a river and looks across to the further shore. Where he stands is dangerous while the other side can be seen to be peaceful but there is no bridge to cross by. So he gathers together logs and creepers and makes himself a raft and then with great effort of hands and feet he gets himself across. When he has reached the further shore he pulls up the raft on dry land and sets off. He does not carry the raft with him!

In the same way, 'this bank' is the round of birth and death beset by the many dangers of dukkha. 'Gazing across to the other shore' means his resolve to practise for the complete elimination of dukkha. 'Gathering the raft's materials' is becoming familiar with the Dhamma by way of thorough study. 'The great effort to cross over' is energetic Dhamma-practice which for most people will include much meditation. 'The Other Shore' is Nibbana.

This simile shows the importance of mundane right view, for it gives the direction for crossing over, and then how with Supermundane Right View the Arahant has put down everything - even the formulations of Dhamma which have been so useful. As remarked in the first chapter (Sec.4) those who are Enlightened have no faith, they know and see Dhamma in themselves. There is nothing to carry and no one to carry it.

4. The Development of Insight (Vipassanā Bhāvana)

Every day, every hour and minute, each second and every moment three things are true for this mind and body:
    All conditioned things are impermanent;
    All conditioned things are dukkha; and
    All dhammas are not self (or not soul).

But how easy it is to forget these things! Though we all know that the body changes continuously, how much aware of this are we? And though mind alters from moment to moment how is our awareness of this? We remember when being reminded of impermance by some experience in life, by a Teacher or by reading a book - and then quickly forget. It is an uncomfortable truth, that conditioned things are impermanent, uncomfortable that is, for those who still cling to pleasure. Those who have seen and felt much suffering are less likely to reject this teaching for they understand that pain and anguish also are impermanent.

'All conditioned things', what does this mean? There is eye and forms, ear and sounds, nose and smells, tongue and tastes, body and touches, mind and mental objects – these are called by the Buddha 'The All' because they are all we can know. All of them arise due to conditions: 'Dependent on eye and forms eye-consciousness arises; the coincidence of the three is contact, with contact as condition arises feeling; with feeling as condition, craving...' In the same way conditions arise and pass away in the case of ear and sounds, and the rest. Not only the exterior senses are conditioned, mind is a play of conditions too where nothing permanent is found. Of course, there seems to be an observer – myself who watches and decides but how can that be true? For when impermanence is contemplated during meditation, the observer disappears. Where has he gone? Has one then lost oneself!

The practical application of 'All conditioned things are impermanent' means that one clings to nothing as lasting or eternal. This teaching leads the earnest practiser to unwrap the layers of craving and clinging to ideas of permanence about people, things, places and doctrines about body and mind too. Whatever is grasped at is a source of dukkha. When nothing is grasped at there is no dukkha.

Here are a few of the verses by a famous nun (*bhikkhuni*) in the Buddha's time, who in her youth had been a beautiful courtesan accompished in many arts:

> Black was my hair, the colour of bees, curled at the ends;
> With ageing it's likened to fibres of hemp –
> not other than this are the Truth-speaker's words.[5]
> Flashing and brilliant as jewels, black and long were my eyes;
> by ageing overwhelmed, no longer beautiful –
> not other than this are the Truth-speaker's words.
> Then were my teeth beautiful, the hue of plantain buds;
> With ageing they have broken and yellowed –
> not other than this are the Truth-speaker's words.
> Full and round were my breasts, close together, lovely and lofty;
> pendulous they hang now as water-skins without water –
> not other than this are the Truth-speaker's words.
> Fair was my body then as a well-burnished tablet of gold;
> Now it is covered all over with very fine wrinkles –
> not other than this are the Truth-speaker's words.
> Lovely both my thighs as the trunks of elephants;
> with ageing they are as a bamboo's stems –
> not other than this are the Truth-speaker's words.
> So was this congeries, decrepit now, abode of dukkha;
> old house with its plaster falling off –
> not other than this are the Truth-speaker's words.

This is the way she reflected on the impermance seen in her body and so won Arahantship.

Though it is true that when one sees a leaf fall from a tree it is a sign of impermanence, yet most people from lack of concentration, do not see it as the impermanence of eye and sight objects. Even when a grey hair appears on the head it is usually only seen as a sign of impermanence, not impermanence itself. A well-concentrated mind which no longer wanders but holds to the subject of meditation is the place to see directly the most subtle aspect of impermanence. Even when there is one-pointedness of mind the moments of attention to the meditation subject arise and pass away. This should be investigated. It should be looked into again and again until the impermanence there becomes apparent.

It is hidden by grasping at permanence, which means at the self-soul concept. As this is gradually loosened so insight into impermanence becomes stronger.

This insight-knowledge differs from knowledge arising from calm meditation in what way? The latter is knowledge about, for instance, visions of what is happening at a distance, or of the devas (deities) and their heavenly abodes, or of what another person is thinking or saying. It could be also knowledge of one's own past lives or how such and such kamma made now by a person will fruit for him in such and such a way. All this knowledge is concerned with the round of birth and death. Insight-knowledge, by contrast, has impermanence, dukkha and not self for its content. It leads, not to further entanglements, but to relinquishment. And it is fresh, new and quite different to what one had known before. Though one now says 'impermanence' and may think that one knows what it is yet when this knowledge arises it is not like that conceptual knowledge at all. It is new and it has the quality of liberation.

The Buddha also called this insight 'direct knowledge', direct, that is, without the intervention of the conceptualizing mind and direct because it gets to the heart of impermanence, dukkha and not self. Non-conceptual thought also arises from calm meditation but it does not concern the investigation of these three subjects essential for liberation.

Insight, in Pali *vipassanā*, is literally 'seeing clearly' and these three are what should be seen. They are called by the Buddha, the Three Characteristics and they mark all living beings. As we know well, all beings are impermanent. As we have to find out, that impermanence extends to every moment of existence. They all experience dukkha, that of birth, decay, disease and death, and the rest - but just 'being' is dukkha due to impermanence. This the finest shade of dukkha to be seen clearly in oneself.

Dukkha has already been described in the last chapter. Though we have much joy and pleasure, even if we experience bliss from our meditation, yet we do not escape dukkha. For all that happiness, gross or subtle, depending on exterior conditions or on interior ones, all without exception is impermanent, it is conditioned, so we may understand something of the truth of 'All conditioned things are dukkha'. And the impermanent cannot be relied upon, it cannot give security and through grasping at it there is dukkha. By having an ungrasping attitude though, there is letting go, a letting-go of much trouble and pain. The Buddha has emphasized this in the verse he spoke concluding his Discourse on the Burden:

70.   *And One's Heart well Purifying*

>   A burden indeed the five aggregates
>   and a person produces his burden,
>   dukkha, the burden that's grasped in the world
>   but happy's discarding the burden;
>   having discarded the burden that's heavy
>   and grasped at no other burden
>   and having pulled craving up with its roots
>   no hunger exists, just Nibbana.[6]

In this verse, the heavy burden of the five aggregates and the person are the same and it is in the aggregate of mental formations that there is the concept of person, self, soul, I and mine. This concept produces the burden, it ensures a plentiful supply of dukkha. The Buddha advises us that we should not only put down the burden we have now, but also we should not take up a new one, that is, grasp at no future life. No grasping means no hunger for more existence and one like this has found the Cool Peace of Nibbana in this very life. After death it is not possible to say anything about such an Enlightened One. What words would fit? (See Chapter VIII)

So we come to the third characteristic, the one hardest to understand and emotionally accept. It is not too difficult to know something of the first two from one's everyday life but this teaching of not self really goes right against the grain of one's self-concepts.

Let us look into this self-concept a little more closely. If we reflect a moment it is easy to see that it does not dwell in the eye, or in forms, or in the eye consciousness. Eye is just a physical organ included in the first aggregate of materiality, and material too is the form. Eye-consciousness which is just the bare visual impression of colour and shape is part of the fifth aggregate of consciousness. The same is true for the other senses, apart from the last, mind. Before looking at the mind if we follow the perceptual process, there is next contact and then feeling - but where is my self in this? He seems to sit just behind the eyes, watching and deciding, but where is he? Perhaps he could be found in the successive processes of recognition, decision, craving, thought conception and discursive thought - but none of these, are permanent, while I feel my self certainly lasts. 'Self' then, is a concept involving all these mental-emotional processes and turns out to be just as impermanent as they are.

If we pursue the analysis of the mind, first there is mind-consciousness which receives the information from the other five senses to which feelings and the recognition process are added as colouring, after which decisions are made about what should be done. (See beginning of Chapter II and the analysis of the causal arising of dukkha in the last Chapter). Where has my self gone in all this?

Yet of course intellectual analysis is not enough for it does not remove the emotional roots of self. These are three in number:- craving, conceit and views. They are expressed in Buddhist works in this way: 'This is mine, I am this, this is my self.'

With thoughts of 'This is mine' - my thoughts, my body, my house... we constantly reinforce the view of self. But what is *mine* really? Possessions and money must be left behind at death. That is where this body stops too. And how much mine is this restless and defiled mind causing so much dukkha? How difficult it is even when one has found a silent and secluded place to experience peace in the mad mind! Even then it jumps all over the place, past, present and future, possible and impossible. So how much mine?

'I am lower, equal or higher, like this or that' so thoughts say and by habitual kamma there arises conviction in those thoughts' truth. But where among all the changing conditions is this 'I'? It should be seen as an impermanent concept. Because there is conceptualizing or conceiving one becomes conceited. One's conceits or concepts of self guarantee conceit arising.[7] And among all concepts the most fundamental is 'I am'. When we speak of a person as 'conceited' we are only indicating the most obvious aspects; the subtle ones are not even noticed, just assumed to be natural. But self would vanish if the concept 'self' also was extinguished and with that concept the raging fire of conceit would go out too. And all the fires of greed, aversion and delusion would be snuffed out. There would then be no more burning with craving, no more smouldering of ignorance. And how marvellous that would be!

'This is my self' is the view I have of my own mind and body. (Notice how language makes for complications!) This aspect of self is the most formulated. Craving is the least so and mostly dependent on feeling, while conceit is more developed and conceptual but does not involve grasping at some view or other. But with views a person supports the self-idea by grasping a belief and then attaching it to himself. 'I believe in ...', or 'My view is like this ...', are typical examples. It may be further supported by quoting the belief of others 'Of course, we believe ...' and it can become very dogmatic and rigid as with the brahmins in the Buddha's days who frequently said of their own teachings 'Only this is true, everything else is false.' Are not such voices to be heard today as well? It is easy to see when views are so near to self, why politics and religion - the usual subjects of views, have been the cause of so much trouble, even murder and wars. 'What I believe must be right, because *I* believe it; and what you believe must be wrong since *I* don't believe it!' This is the terrible tangle of self. What dukkha has it not been responsible for?

How can this not-self-nature of the five aggregates be penetrated? By always questioning 'Who? - as one stands, walks, sits or lies down. By not taking these actions for granted but questioning the fundamental assumption which is usually made, that is, repeatedly reflecting 'Where is this self?' in both physical and mental actions. Though such inquiry may begin in a verbal way it progresses to a non-verbal stage where there is just questioning - 'Who sees, hears, smells, tastes, touches, thinks?'

In Zen Buddhism this technique has been formulated in several koans, such as 'Who drags this corpse around?'. The emphasis in this case is always on the question - 'Who?' which will produce mental states not satisfied with the usual answer 'Well I am of course!' 'Who' and 'Where' should be used intensively to examine every dhamma, each momentary experience as it arises and passes away, for any sign of 'self' or 'soul'.

This brings us back to the Buddha's words: 'All dhammas are not self'. Why did the Buddha use the word 'conditioned things' (sankhārā) when speaking of impermanence and dukkha but 'dhammas' when referring to not self? The range of meaning in the word 'dhamma' is wider than that of 'conditioned things'. The former includes the latter calling them 'conditioned dhammas' (saṅkhata-dhammā) but also covers the Unconditioned Dhamma which is Nibbana. So not only are all conditions things - all elements of body and mind, not self but also the Unconditioned is not self too. This means that theories about the Unconditioned being the True Self, Cosmic Self, or whatever other self-term may be used, can have no basis in the Buddha's Teaching. When such words are used and when experiences are fitted to such words there is still grasping at self, an extended and refined self or soul no doubt, but still it is self/soul. 'All dhammas should not be clung to'[8] says the Buddha. Nibbana, the ultimate freedom should not be seen as any sort of self. In fact, it is only rightly known by direct knowledge or insight when all the five aggregates are seen as not self. 'Therefore, monks, any form, feeling, perception, mental formations and consciousness whatsoever, whether past, future or present, in oneself or external, coarse or fine, inferior or superior, far or near, should all be regarded as it actually is by right understanding thus: This is not mine, I am not this, this is not my self', so the Buddha said in his second discourse.

Anatta or not self is a synonym of voidness. The Buddha explained the saying 'Void is the world' in this way: 'It is void of self and what belongs to self. And what is void of self and what belongs to self? The eye, forms, eye-consciousness, eye-contact, any feeling born of eye contact. (The same is said for ear, nose, tongue and body). The mind, mental objects, mind-consciousness, mind-contact, any feeling born of mind-contact is void of self and what belongs to self.' So the nature of all dhammas is voidness, they have no being upon which can be built a theory of self. Later Buddhist scholasticism has departed from the Buddha's radical teachings that no dhammas should be clung to as they are all void, with theories of the self-natures of different dhammas. This is, of course, just holding views instead of getting on with practice. The result of this was that an opposition party arose calling themselves Mahāyāna which proclaimed all dhammas as void but linked this doctrine to the concept of the bodhisattva who will save all beings. This effort to prove that the Bodhisattva was superior to the Arahant could only be made on the basis of scholastic misinterpretations and by ignoring the Buddha's words, 'All dhammas are not self'. This tangle of views has had repercussions which still cause misunderstanding down to our days. It has even led the followers of Mahayana to assert that the Arahants, those who according to the Pali discourses know for themselves 'Birth is exhausted, the Holy Life has been lived out, what was to be done is done, there is no more of this to come', have still to be reborn as Bodhisattvas as they have still a subtle 'covering' left in the mind - all of which is quite contrary to the earliest Buddhist tradition!

As the Buddha said frequently, views are limitless in number - and certainly Buddhists have produced their share of them! His own words which we reproduce below and the statements of great Enlightened Teachers of meditation living now in Thailand and Burma, are like a bright shining lamp compared to the dark jungles of self views.

'Monks, the possession that one might possess, that were permanent, everlasting - do you see any such possession ?' 'No Lord.' 'The self-theory - clinging whereby one might cling that would never arouse sorrow, lamentation, pain, grief and despair in him who clung thereby; do you see any such self-theory-clinging?' 'No, Lord'. 'The view as support that one might take as support that would never arouse sorrow and so on in him who took it as support; do you see any such view as support?' 'No, Lord'. 'Monks, there being self would there be what belongs to self?' 'Yes, Lord'. 'And there being what belongs to self would there be self?' 'Yes, Lord'. 'Monks, self and what belongs to self being inapprehensible as true and established, then would not this view "This is the world, this the self; after death I shall be permanent, everlasting, eternal, not subject to change, I shall endure as long as eternity" be the pure perfection of a fool's idea?' 'How could it not be, Lord? It would be the pure perfection of a fool's idea'[9]

Clinging to a self-(soul-) theory is one type of clinging (*upādāna*) which is abandoned on the path of insight. Clinging regarding sensual desires, existence (literally 'being') and views are also completely unwrapped. This does of course mean radical and drastic changes in the person who experiences true insight or *vipassanā*. If no changes take place though one practises some meditation path which may be called 'vipassanā' one has not experienced the real thing. In every case vipassanā must concern impermanence, dukkha and not self and the effect of this direct knowledge on the meditator must be a reduction of defilements and lessening of conceit along with a strengthened mindfulness and greater purity of mind-heart.

Though later scholasticism has classifed insight into stages, this is not a feature of the Buddha's original teaching. Such 'stages' can be a very dangerous thing, especially when there are books available actually detailing the physical and mental-emotional 'symptoms' of each stage. As with the jhanas, meditators can then start feeling, 'Now I have reached this level of insight, now that ...' - a fine thing for conceit, the very factor that real insight lessens. So these stages have not been given here and meditators are advised to disregard them and just get on with however much practice they can do each day. Then it will be most helpful to have the guidance of a good Teacher who has gone further along the Path, or reached its end, for the subtle instructions needed for disentangling the cravings, conceits and views tangle on which the self-conceit rests.

NOTES TO CHAPTER IV

[1] For this aspect see *Lay Buddhist Practice*, Wheel No. 206-207, B.P.S., Kandy.

[2] All translations in this section are those of Ven. Nyanamoli Thera modified from *The Life of the Buddha* and *A Treasury of the Buddha's Words*, both from B.P.S., Kandy.

[3] The first is just the word 'Buddha' - Enlightened One, in the nominative case. The second, 'Perfect Destroyer of Defilements' and the last 'Homage to the Liberated Ones, Homage to Liberation'.

[4] Impermanence, Dukkha, Not-self.

[5] The Truth-speaker is the Buddha who has taught the Noble Truths, or whose Dhamma is entirely truthful.

[6] Literally 'having quite cooled down' or 'having Nibbana-ed'.

[7] In Pali too the play on words is also made, which is not accidental of course, between *Māna* (concept, 'conceit') and *maññati* to conceptualize, conceive.

[8] *Sabbe dhamma nālaṁ abhinivesāya.*

[9] Quotations in this section are mostly from *The Life of the Buddha*, Bhikkhu Nyanamoli, (B.P.S., Kandy), with some changes.

And One's Heart well Purifying

V

MEDITATION METHODS

In this chapter only five meditation subjects will be described, though traditionally there are forty.[1] Many of these are little used or only occasionally employed in special circumstances. Those which are given here are the commonest meditation subjects used in Buddhist countries at the present time. Two of them, Loving-kindness and the Recollection of the Buddha, lead when developed to calm alone, that is to the jhanas. The other three, Mindfulness of Breathing, Walking and the Contemplation of Unattractiveness lead both to calm and to insight.

The difference between these two groups of meditation subjects becomes clearer when one considers that in the case of the first two an effort has to be made constantly to focus the mind-heart upon them, they are not usually something naturally present all the time. In the case of the last three however, they require mindfulness to be directed at what is actually going on - breathing, walking or unattractiveness. This is the characteristic which they share with most of the exercises in the Discourse on the Foundations of Mindfulness described in Chapter Three.

While the emphasis in the last two chapters has been on describing the Dhamma rather theoretically, in this one its practical aspects are emphasized. We shall try to answer the question, 'How can I practise...?' these different types of meditation.

1. Loving-Kindness (Metta):

Anyone who wishes to start meditating on Metta must be prepared to make an effort with their treatment of things, animals and people in everyday life.

The things that one uses or handles should be treated gently, not roughly. If one is to be restrained from roughness in mind - any kind of antipathy, one should take care over roughness of body and speech. The Buddha exhorted the troublesome Band of Six monks whose conduct was certainly not well restrained, not to make a loud clatter or talk roughly - such actions indicate a rough mind. In daily life then, rough bodily actions refer to slamming doors, putting things down with a clatter, as well as that kind of bustle which is born out of hatred. It is good to be energetic but not 'speedy' if that arises because of others' slowness. Having compared others with oneself (conceit), one then bustles about (expressing aversion). A fine mixture of defilements! Bodily roughness is also seen in the hardness of one's face - there is no smile there. The cure for all this is obvious but needs mindfulness.

Speech should not be rough either, so harsh speech should be avoided and then one will be practising one aspect of the Noble Eightfold Path. Harsh speech includes any kind of hurtful words whether one is openly angry or inwardly resentful. Both roughness of body and speech may be expressed without a person being aware that anything is wrong. These ways of action may be habitual, thought if it is so few friends and much trouble may be expected. And it is impossible to be rid of mental roughness, that is, aversion, without making an effort with these two expressions of it.

It is good practice, if one is angry with someone to restrain oneself from saying anything to him, or writing anything, until one's heart has cooled down. When one feels calm inside the difficulty, whatever it was, can be seen more clearly and then a calm conversation with that person may be possible and a resolution of that trouble. Impetuosity is on the side of anger and has nothing to commend it.

Towards all animals as far as this is practicable one should be gentle. They want to live as one desires to do, they do not want more dukkha. In their lives they have more dukkha already than human beings and much less that they can do about it. No more dukkha should be added to their lives by us!

Regarding other people, one who desires to increase loving-kindness should be as kind and helpful as possible and always speak friendly and comforting words. A cheerful 'Good Morning' is a good way to start the day mindful of its meaning, 'May you have a good morning'. A smile can also convey loving-kindness. And if a smile is going to look too much at variance with one's feelings and so too artificial, a few calmly-spoken pleasant words would be better. It is really not much use only window-dressing when in the shop the goods are all rotten! It is necessary to deal with one's heart through meditation while at the same time making the sort of effort described above.

What about the theory which says 'You should get anger out of your system by confronting the other person involved'? This seems to rest on the assumption that 'the other person makes me angry'. But really this is not true at all. When he is angry, that is his anger; it is his own fire of aversion burning him and he owns the Kamma he is making, so why do I become angry too? Do I want to burn as well? Anger is like the bushfire leaping from tree to tree, for when one person's heart is ablaze the tinder in another's catches fire. The tinder is the underlying tendency to aversion. There is no advantage for me when my heart catches fire, only more dukkha. Confrontations usually result in this. They may begin by being peaceful enough but enmity soon starts to operate, after it follow accusations and then there is quarrel. There is no way to develop loving-kindness here!

And then what about 'righteous anger'? Maybe one sees a child being mistreated by its parents; is it not then right to be angry and do something? If it is possible to intervene peacefully, that is good. But any intervention fuelled by anger will not result in good for any of the parties involved. It will only make such a situation worse. Firmness is needed at such a time, not anger, and a person whose

Meditation Methods

mind, speech and body actions are firm and decisive will succeed where the 'righteously' angry person could not. Anger is always unwholesome and is never justified in the Buddha's teaching. It is even more blame-worthy when anger is expressed about religious matters, since Dhamma is for quelling anger and the other defilements.

Seeking forgiveness, if it is done by both people towards each other, is effective. Buddhist monks frequently use a formula like this to ask the pardon of other monks who they may have wronged, if only in mind: 'Whatever has been done with carelessness by mind, speech and body towards the Venerable one, for all those faults please pardon me, Sir.' This produces harmony in the Sangha. Something similar would help in ending enmity in lay society.

Helpfulness is also a practical expression of loving-kindness. If one sees what should be done in any situation, then lend a hand willingly. This means that wherever one goes one looks round to see if any help is required before sitting down or resting oneself. This is an important way of training oneself to make an effort too. But care is needed that one's 'helpfulness' is not that kind of bustle arising from aversion which has been mentioned already. Such busy-ness can easily increase tensions.

The Buddha recommended the four bases of sympathy for development in every-day life: *giving, kindly speech, beneficial actions* and *impartiality*. All of them make for the growth of loving-kindness if practised in the right way, as well as for the increase in the number of one's friends. There is little need to *explain* these things but much need to *practise* them.

After this review of the practical aspects of loving-kindness in everyday life and before going on to review methods of cultivating loving-kindness as a meditation, here are some methods of dealing with aversion.

There are nine such methods recommended in the Commentaries, which may be labelled as follows: Seeing lack of Dhamma-practice in oneself; seeing the good in the person for whom one has enmity; seeing how anger harms oneself; seeing that both oneself and the enemy are the owners of their own kammas; contemplation of the Buddha's virtues in past lives; recollecting that all beings have been one's parents and relatives; recollecting the advantages of practising loving-kindness; inquiring 'Who are you angry with? the head-hairs? etc.; and giving a gift.

(A) SEEING LACK OF DHAMMA-PRACTICE IN ONESELF:

The following passages from the Discourses are suitable for reflection:[2] 'Monks, if bandits brutally severed limb from limb with a two-handled saw, he who entertained hate in his heart on that account would not be one who carried out my teaching.' If no hatred was felt at such a time this would indeed be the perfection of loving-kindness! How much more Dhamma-practice one has to do to reach this standard!

Or there are some verses worth reflecting on:

78.   *And One's Heart well Purifying*

> To repay angry men in kind
> is worse than to be angry first;
> repay not angry men in kind
> and win a battle hard to win.
> The weal of both he does promote,
> his own and then the other's too,
> who shall another's anger know
> and mindfully maintain his peace.

Finally, the Discourse on the Wretchedness of Anger may be quoted in brief:

> Monks, there are seven things gratifying and helpful to an enemy that befall one who is angry, whether a woman or a man. What seven? Here, monks, an enemy wishes thus for his enemy: 'Let him be ugly'. Why is that? No enemy relishes an enemy's beauty. Now when this person is angry, a prey to anger, ruled by anger, be he ever so well-bathed and well-anointed, with hair and beard trimmed and clothed in white, yet he is ugly through his being a prey to anger. This is the first thing gratifying and helpful to an enemy that befalls one who is angry, whether a woman or a man. Furthermore, an enemy wishes thus for his enemy, 'Let him lie in pain' ... 'Let him have no good fortune' ... 'Let him not be wealthy' ... 'Let him not be famous' ... 'Let him have no friends' ... 'Let him not, on the break up of the body, after death, reappear in a happy destiny, in the heavenly world'. Why is that? No enemy relishes an enemy's going to a happy destiny. Now when this person is angry, a prey to anger, ruled by anger, he misconducts himself in body, speech and mind. Misconducting himself thus, on the break up of the body after death, he reappears in a state of deprivation, in an unhappy destiny, in perdition, in hell, through his being prey to anger.[3]

After reflecting in this way one can only conclude that much is still to be done and that anger is both a root of unwholesomeness and a hindrance - surely an evil worth giving up!

(B) SEEING GOOD IN THE PERSON FOR WHOM ONE HAS ENMITY:

A mind ruled by aversion has the characteristic of noting faults in others. This is the drain-inspector's mind always looking for the worst and even delighting in it. Such a mind is constantly critical in a destructive way, always pulling others to pieces - and usually getting a fine ego-boost in the process. All this is opposite to loving-kindness. Hear what the Buddha has to say:

> The faults of others are easy to see,
> hard indeed to see are one's own,
> and so one winnows just like chaff
> the faults of other people, while
> hiding indeed those of one's own,

> as a crafty cheat the losing throw.
> Whoso sees others's faults,
> taking offence, censorious,
> for him pollutions ever grow;
> he is far from destroying them[4]

The method recommended here is to consider the virtues of the person one is annoyed with and to ignore the faults. Whatever is admirable in that other person, whatever they do well, indeed better than one can do oneself, all such qualities should be considered as soon as mindfulness knows that there is enmity present.

(C) SEEING HOW ANGER HARMS ONESELF.

A poem from the Commentaries gives plenty of food for thought:

> Suppose an enemy has hurt
> you now, in what is his domain,
> why try yourself as well to hurt
> your mind? - That is not his domain.
> In tears you left your family,[5]
> they had been kind and helpful too.
> So why not leave your enemy,
> the anger that brings harm to you?
> This anger that you entertain
> is gnawing at the very roots
> of all the virtues that you guard -
> Who is there such a fool as you?
> Another does ignoble deeds,
> so you are angry - how is this?
> Do you then want to copy too
> the sort of acts that he commits?
> Suppose another, to annoy,
> provokes you with some odious act,
> why suffer anger to spring up
> and do as he would have you do?
> If you get angry, then may be
> you make *him* suffer, may be not:
> though with the hurt that anger brings
> *you* certainly are punished now.
> If anger-blinded enemies
> set out to tread the path of woe,
> do you by getting angry too
> intend to follow heel to toe?
> If hurt is done you by a foe
> because of anger on your part,
> then put your anger down, for why
> should you be harassed groundlessly?
> Since states last but a moment's time
> those aggregates, by which was done
> the odious act, have ceased, so now
> what is it you are angry with?[6]

> Whom shall he hurt, who seeks to hurt
> another, in the other's absence?
> *Your* presence is the cause of hurt;
> Why are you angry then with *him*?

These verses emphasize where the hateful is to be found; in one's own heart, not in others.

(D) UNDERSTANDING OWNERSHIP OF KAMMA:

A part of Buddhist daily practice is to recollect these words of the Buddha:

> I am the owner of my Kamma, the heir to my Kamma, born of my Kamma, related to my Kamma, abide supported by my Kamma; whatever kamma I shall do, whether good or evil, of that I shall be the heir. Beings (he, she, they) are the owners of their kamma, heirs to their kamma, born of their kamma, related to their kamma, abide supported by their kamma; whatever kamma they will do, whether good or evil, of that they will be the heirs.

Anger and resentment can be allayed if one brings this passage to mind for one then becomes mindful that the dust one flings against others returns to dirty oneself, and if one spits upwards the spittle falls only on oneself. As the Buddha said:

> Whoso offends an inoffensive man,
> an innocent and blameless man,
> Upon that fool evil turns
> as fine dust thrown against the wind.[7]

(E) CONTEMPLATION OF THE BODHISATTA'S DEEDS:

Another way to achieve the stilling of anger is to remember how the Bodhisatta, who in after lives would become the Buddha Gotama, behaved towards those who tormented him. Is there any unkind word or act that one could not bear after reading and remembering this story?[8]

A long time ago the Bodhisatta was a hermit living in the forest outside Benares or Kasi as it was sometimes called. There he had a hut and dwelt many peaceful years in meditation. And when people came to visit him, he received them courteously and talked Dhamma with them, especially about patience. Then as people heard from him the benefits of patience expounded in so many different ways and with such good illustrations, they forgot his original name and called him just Khantivādi; the Preacher of Patience.

One day in the hot season the King of Benares decided to have an outing in the country and ordered preparations to be made.

The parkland was cleared and decorated, the city suitably cleaned and adorned and the elephants caparisoned. On the appointed day his majesty with the full pomp of royalty, attended by his royal guard of amazons and followed by a procession of ministers, and his greater and lesser wives, all mounted on elephants, went through the throngs of citizens paying their respects to the cool shade of the park.

There he was entertained with music and dancing, with sports in the water and with feasting and drinking, so that he became quite drunk. The ladies of his harem seeing him snore, said 'Why should we weary ourselves to amuse him? Let us explore the forest!' So leaving him guarded by his amazons, the leader of whom held the royal sword, they wandered off chattering, laughing and picking flowers. Following a track in the woods they came eventually to the hut of the Preacher of Patience. Seeing him with long grey hair and beard sitting in tranquil silence, they ceased their playfulness and paid their respects to him. When he emerged from meditation, he offered them water and forest fruits and then began to discourse to them on patience, giving such good examples and explaining points so well that they were totally absorbed in his words.

Meanwhile, the king awoke, bleary-eyed and irritable. Staring round he demanded to know where his royal wives had gone to - and when he was informed he snatched his sword and set off in pursuit. In a short time he arrived at the hermitage and was enraged to see his wives paying him no attention at all.

The Preacher of Patience was at that time exhorting the ladies with one hand raised in gentle admonition. The furious king shouting 'We shall find where you keep your patience!' sliced of the Teacher's hand. The latter calmly replied, 'Your majesty, you seem to think that patience is in that hand, whereas of course, it dwells in the heart'. Though others tried to restrain him and though his frightened wives fled from the place, the king maddened by liquor and hatred continued to hack the Bodhisatta's body to pieces. When he had dismembered him so that he had no arms or legs and no ears or nose the king rushed away. It is said that the earth was unable to bear the weight of such terrible Kamma and opening, swallowed him up.

The king's ministers meanwhile approached the dying Teacher and begged him not to curse the whole land (for the rishis of old were much feared because of the supposed power of their intense rage) but to damn only the late king who had tortured him. The Bodhisatta replied, 'May the king live long in happiness! I curse no one at all. May all beings be happy!' - and so he died.

> In ancient days there was a sage,
> of patience he was a paragon,
> he kept his patience even when
> the King of Kasi quartered him.

(F) RECOLLECTING ALL BEINGS AS ONE'S PARENTS:

Those who have confidence in the teaching on rebirth can also recollect this passage: 'Monks, it is not easy to find a being who has not formerly been your mother, father, brother, sister, son or daughter in this incalculable round of birth and death.' When the affections one has for one's mother or father, or any other relative - and one should only recollect mother and father in this case if they have been loving and understanding - is awoken towards other people then anger subsides. Carefully consider how much care and trouble one's dear (mother, father or whoever) took with one's upbringing and then think: This one too that I have become upset with, he (she, they) have also been my dear relatives. They have helped me so much and now how can I think ill of them?

(G) RECOLLECTING THE ADVANTAGES OF LOVING-KINDNESS:

There are eleven of these listed by the Buddha: 'Happily one goes to sleep, happy one awakes, one sees no evil dreams, one is dear to human beings, and dear to non-humans, the devas (gods) protect one, fire, poison and weapons do not harm one, quickly one's mind is concentrated, the expression on one's face is serene, one dies unconfused, and even if one penetrates no higher one will be reborn in the Brahma world.' These will be explained at the end of this section.

(H) INQUIRING 'WHO ARE YOU ANGRY WITH?'

Recollect impermanence: 'That person has now changed completely, mind and body - what can I be angry with there?' Or recollect the parts of the body (see under Unattractiveness in this chapter): 'Am I angry with head-hair, body-hair, nails, teeth or skin...?' By some such method one finds out that one is not angry with that person, who is dissolved away by analysis, but with one's own ideas and feelings. This is one good reason for starting loving-kindness towards oneself.

(I) GIVING A GIFT:

This is a method which may be tried specially when other ways do not work. If a gift is to break down the barriers of aversion to others in oneself, or the aversion of others to oneself, it must be well-given. This means, as whole-heartedly as possible, with a pleasant face and polite manner at a time when currents of aversion are not running high. It should also be a gift which is of some value to oneself; obviously it is no good throwing away rubbish and expecting this to heal enmity, and it must be something which the receiver will value highly too. Care should be taken in the decoration of the gift and the way that it is given. As much mindfulness and wisdom should be employed in giving gifts for this purpose as one can muster. The results often exceed one's expectations.

Starting the practice with oneself is emphasized in the Buddha's Discourse on Loving-Kindness which begins: 'This must be done to

Meditation Methods

gain the State of Peace' - and then follow fifteen items which are useful as supports for the growth of loving-kindness. We shall briefly look at them, one by one.[9]
First, one should be *able*, that is capable and not lazy, diligent and not negligent, for what can be gained by the slothful? *Upright* comes next, that is, all one's actions (*kammas*) of body and speech should accord with the precepts; this is paired with *straight*, or having a mind truly in accord with Dhamma where effort and mindfulness help to be aware of defilements and so to be rid of them. And one should be *not proud*. Pride is a common disease of those who undertake a path of development, specially where this depends on one's own practice, not on others' grace. *Easy to speak to* is next on the list and goes along with the last, since it means that one can be corrected easily, that one is humble and will not blurt out recriminations or find excuses, but just accept good words of advice such as a Teacher speaks. The Buddha said:

> If as a broken gong
> you don't reverberate,
> recrimination not in you:
> here, Nibbana you have attained.[10]

And then of course one will be *mild* and gentle, not given to rough actions, to harsh criticism or to angry thoughts, just the sort of person who one would expect to grow in loving-kindness. Next on the list is *well-content*, for envy is the enemy of one who is not contented, and that is just a relation of aversion. Laypeople cannot practise contentment with little as can monks and nuns but in these days of proliferation of goods and enjoyments some contentment is necessary if one is to remain sane. *Easily satisfied* literally is 'easy to support' so one should not be demanding of others' time and wealth but rather accept whatever comes, again easier for those who have left their homes for the homeless life than for householders. A similar factor is *not caught up in too much bustle* - not having work that exhausts one or too many things to do - as many people actually prefer so that they have no time to look at their own dukkha. *Frugal in one's ways* also comes easier to homeless monks and nuns but has its application to lay life too. However, it does not imply being mean! Generous to others and frugal oneself is what is meant. *With senses calmed*, a difficult thing in lay life where there are so many pleasures and distractions. Still, the lay meditator will soon get to know what sense-pleasures stir up the mind! Then comes *intelligent*, for a confused person will not realize what things cause the mind to be upset but one should also be *not bold*. Intelligence often goes hand-in-hand with arrogance, or boldness in the bad sense of the word. One should not be like a crow, beady-eyed to get something out of everything, nor strut and display oneself as the crow does. *Unswayed by the emotions of the crowd* is rather a loose translation as it refers also to getting things out of people by sorrowing when they sorrow and by happiness when they are happy. Loving-kindness does not arise in the heart of one who is concerned with a host of exterior things, the motivations for which are usually greed, aversion and delusion. Last comes *abstaining from the ways that wise men blame*: notice that 'wise men' are mentioned - one should not abstain from what fools blame for they see blame where there is none while practising what is blameworthy because it is unwholesome and causes harm.

Now, coming to the methods of meditation: these may be preceded by or incorporate various chants on the subject of loving-kindness. Here is a selection. First, a translation of some Pali verses traditionally recited in Sri Lanka written by some unknown practiser in the past;

> Having seen that like oneself
> all being seek for happiness,
> patiently then cultivate
> love for beings all.
> Ever happy may I be,
> may I from dukkha e'er be free,
> with friends and neutral ones also,
> may my foes be happy too.
> Within the boundaries of this town
> may beings ever happy be,
> likewise those from foreign lands
> and men from other galaxies.
> From all around the galaxies,
> all creatures and all breathing things,
> all persons and all entities,
> be happy in their destinies.
> Likewise women, men as well,
> the Noble Ones, the unawake,
> devas, men, unhappy ones,
> who in the ten directions dwell.

These verses outline the direction of loving-kindness practice, about which more will be said below: first towards oneself, then towards the different categories of friends, neutral persons and enemies, afterwards spreading it directionally to cover certain areas and finally including all classes of beings when loving-kindness becomes infinite in the ten directions (of north, north-east, etc. plus the zenith and nadir).

A simple Pali-English chant, also originally from Sri Lanka, again emphasizes that one starts with oneself, while giving some thoughts which can be the basis for loving-kindness:-

> Ahaṁ avero homi -
> May I be free from enmity (pause)
>
> Abyāpajjho homi -
> May I be free from hurtfulness (p)
>
> Anīgho homi -
> May I be free from troubles of mind and body (p)

Sukhī attānaṁ pariharāmi -
May I be able to protect my own happiness (p)

Sabbe sattā -
Whatever beings there are

Averā hontu -
May they be free from enmity (p)

Sabbe sattā -
Whatever beings there are

Abyāpajjhā hontu -
May they be free from hurtfulness (p)

Sabbe sattā -
Whatever beings there are

Anīghā hontu -
May they be free from troubles of mind and body (p)

Sabbe sattā -
Whatever beings there are

Sukhī attānaṁ -
May they be able to protect their own happiness.

In this passage 'enmity' is *thoughts* of aversion while 'hurtfulness' covers actions of body and speech rooted in that aversion. How one protects one's own happiness and that of others has already been illustrated in the story of the acrobat and his girl apprentice; it will be further clarified by King Pasenadi's reflections on the good of oneself which are related below.

The recitation of the Buddha's famous 'Discourse of Loving-kindness which should be practised' is done thousands of time daily in Buddhist countries. Here is a metrical English version for those who do not know Pali:-

> (1) What should be done by one who's skilled in wholesomeness
> to gain the State of Peacefulness is this:
> One must be able, upright, straight and not proud,
> easy to speak to, mild and well-content,
> easily satisfied and not caught up
> in too much bustle,
> and frugal in one's ways,
> with senses calmed, intelligent, not bold,
> unswayed by the emotions of the crowd,
> abstaining from the ways that wise men blame;
> (and this the thought that one should always hold;)

And One's Heart well Purifying

(2) May beings all live happily and safe
and may their hearts rejoice within themselves.
Whatever there may be with breath of life,
whether they be frail or very strong,
without exception, be they long or short,
or middle-sized, or be they big or small,
or thick or visible or invisible
or whether they dwell far or they dwell near,
those that are here, those seeking to exist;
may beings all rejoice within themselves.
Let no one bring about another's ruin,
or him despise in any way or place;
let them not wish each other any ill
from provocation or from enmity.

(3) Just as a mother at the risk of life
loves and protects her son, her only son,
so let him cultivate this boundless love
to all that live in the whole universe;
extending from a consciousness sublime
upwards and downwards and across the world,
untroubled, free of hate and enmity.
And while he stands and while he walks and sits
or he lies down still free from drowsiness,
let him be intent on this mindfulness:
this is Divine Abiding here they say,

(4) But when he lives quite free from any view,
is virtuous, with perfect insight won,
and greed for sensual desires expelled –
he surely comes no more to any womb.

The fifteen factors in the first part of this discourse have been commented on already. After them (2), follows the kinds of thoughts which should be cultivated. Something will be said about them below. The next section, (3) outlines the results of practice, first by comparing loving-kindness to a mother's tender love for her only child. This kind of love which never causes harm to others should be extended to all beings in all states of existence. (It is interesting here to note that the Buddha has avoided comparing loving-kindness to the love of lovers as often found in spiritual traditions. As Ven Nyanamoli remarks[11] – this 'is often conceived as a consuming flame, and then it sometimes aspires to purification through torture and the violence of martydom'). A mother's love is much nearer to the ideal of Metta than lovers' love because the former is so much more unselfish. See the remarks too on kāma in Chapter III. 3.

While kāma is limited, mettā can become unlimited through its extension in jhana. Then the whole world, the whole universe even, is irradiated with loving-kindness. The passage from the Discourses below also shows the way this can be done. The last part of the Discourse, (4), is a reminder that loving-kindness even when practised to jhana-level will not lead to liberation, a point that devotees, Buddhist or otherwise, need to bear in mind. Though one's gentleness is as great as the universe and though one has therefore liberated one's heart of narrow passions, still self-concept and views endure, still there is subtle attachment to being-becoming, so the liberation by wisdom has to be developed as well.

The last passage which we shall give here is an oft-repeated formula on the development of jhana through loving-kindness.

'Someone here abides with heart endued with loving-kindness extending over one quarter, likewise the second, likewise the third, likewise the fourth, and so above, below, around and everywhere, and to all as to himself; he abides with his heart abundant with loving-kindness, exalted, measureless, without hostility or ill-will extending over the all-encompassing universe.'

This passage is the basis for developing loving-kindness in the directional method which will be explained below. Complete success with this way can be seen in modern times with the accounts of Venerable Acariya Mun's loving-kindness which was said by those who could perceive it to spread through the universe and to all planes of existence.[12]

Now we come to how loving-kindness should be developed while sitting in meditation. Loving other beings is only successful when one loves oneself in the right way. Loving oneself means a relative absence of conflicts and self-hatred. It is implied in the words of the chant above: 'May I be able to protect my own happiness.' This is best protected by making good kamma, as much as possible and as frequently as possible. The love of oneself was spoken of by King Pasenadi when he went to see the Buddha:[13]

> When, lord, I had retired and was alone this was the reflection that arose in my mind: Who loves himself? Who does not love himself? And then, lord, I thought: Those who practise wrong conduct by body, speech and mind, they do not love themselves. Even though they should say, 'We love ourselves' yet they do not love themselves. What is the reason? They do to themselves what a hater would do to one he hates. Therefore they do not love themselves. But those who practise good conduct by body, speech and mind, they love themselves. Even though they should say, 'We do not love ourselves', yet they do love themselves. What is the reason? They do to themselves what a friend would do to a friend. Therefore, they love themselves.

The Buddha agreed completely with the king's observation. This love is emphasized too by one of the Buddha's sayings:-

> I visited all quarters with my mind
> nor found I any dearer than myself;
> self is likewise to every other dear;
> who loves himself will never harm another.[14]

To promote this true love of oneself, when seated in meditation try to find the feeling of warm friendliness in the region of one's heart. The meditator should try to go down to the heart and find this feeling and then spread it throughout the body. If no feeling of this sort can be found then use words repeated silently to oneself such as 'May I be happy, may I be at peace, may I be secure', until such feeling is produced. It is important to get out of one's head and down in the body. Loving-kindness which is in the head is only a matter of words. If still there is no feeling of love, then try this visualization: See a white lotus bud in the heart and when this is steady, make it open up and from its centre rays of golden light appear. Let this light, which will stimulate the feeling, be spread thought the body.

How long one spends on oneself must depend on personal circumstances but it is not much use going on to others before some metta is established towards oneself. Good friends are always the people to start with but not anyone with whom one has sexual relations. It is better not to include such a person in a loving-kindness meditation as the metta can turn into kama or sensual love, which is called the 'near enemy', against which one has to guard. Do not switch from one friend to another too quickly. Each person should be given several minutes before changing to the next. And it is advisable to practise loving-kindness using the same friends in the same order each day for then the mind gets used to a pattern. It should be possible after a time to notice less tension in oneself and more love in everyday life for those friends to whom one practises.

When loving-kindness flows smoothly towards them, one may go on to neutral people, just bare acquaintances, for whom one feels neither love nor enmity. The feeling-tone should be maintained the same as for the friends. If it is not the same then more work needs to be done on metta to one's friends. Success with neutral people can be judged from how one greets them and treats them in one's life. It is possible to get many more friends in this way!

After neutral people have been irradiated in this way, lastly turn to those for whom one feels enmity. Great care is needed here that while focusing on such people, either visually or using their names, that ill-will does not arise and shatter the loving-kindness. This is the 'far-enemy', the opposite of loving-kindness, which one has always to guard against. Quickly return to reviewing one's friends if this should happen.

Eventually, friends, neutral people and enemies are all seen to be the same and can be viewed with love in the same way and treated lovingly too. From particular persons the mind can then go on to the pervasion of directions and different sorts of beings with loving-kindness, thus developing in the way of jhana. One can always know if metta practice goes well since it will become wordless but feelingful.

The last method is widely used but three others also are effective for some people. The first of these is the directional spread of loving-kindness. Having established metta in oneself then pervade each of the six directions beginning with all the beings in front of oneself. Words or feelings may be used but the latter are more effective. One feels as though all the beings in the direction one faces are being pervaded with metta, as far distant and as strongly as one can manage. After some minutes, turn attention to all beings upon one's right side, then behind one, left side, below and above. This method of pervading the six directions can be used as a supplementary meditation to one's main subject, either practising it for ten to fifteen minutes before or at the end of the sitting period.

If it is possible to spread out loving-kindness spatially, that is extending one's mind-heart of loving-kindness over say first, a room, then a house, afterwards several houses, a street, city and so on, then this is a second form of practice. But as with the method above one must not deceive oneself, as the man did who practised 'boundless' metta every day and then swore at his servant, a story to be related in the next chapter.

The last method is by way of different groups of beings. To practise this some confidence is needed in the various possibilities for rebirth as taught by the Buddha. Usually three groups are used; All devas (divinities, gods), all human beings, all unhappy ones (in the subhuman realms including ghosts, animals and hells.) Human beings may be divided into women and men, Noble Ones and ordinary people, making six groups altogether. This way may be practised combined with the ten directions (east, west, north, south, southeast...zenith and nadir), changing each line and meditating silently for a minute or two, beginning thus:

'May all women in the eastern direction be happy' (western, northern, etc.)

May all men in the eastern direction be happy ...' etc.

With one minute of meditation for each of these categories, a full hour goes by! This type of meditation is very suitable for beginners and those with badly distracted minds. It is also very helpful for people who have strong aversion or resentment. It may be shortened, using only the first three categories, (devas, humans, unhappy ones), or these three may be employed with a longer time given to each directional division. The wording can also be changed if one feels more loving-kindness results from 'be free from enmity', 'be free from hurtfulness', 'be free from troubles of mind and body', instead of 'be happy'. A very effective meditation, especially when the chanting of each line is made as evocative of loving-kindness as possible.

So far, loving-kindness has been emphasized as a quality to be practised in relation to other human beings. Indeed, it could not be called metta if confined to a sentimental tenderness to animals. But is is important that they are also suffused with loving-kindness for when this is done one has no need to fear any animal, even fierce carnivores or poisonous creatures. They will not attack someone who has a strong heart of metta. Many stories are told, some of which are found in the *Life of Phra Acharn Mun, Meditation Master*, of tigers that did not trouble meditating monks. To this day in Thailand monks who meditate are rarely troubled by snakes or other deadly animals and so can live peacefully in a cave and at the foot of a tree without fear. If a person has such fear of animals, say snakes or even of spiders, then the following chant with some meditation to follow it will be effective:

My love to the Virupakkhas[15]
and to the Erapathas too,
my love to the Chabyaputtas
and to the black Gotamas too.
My love to those with no feet,
to those with two feet, my love too,
my love to those with four feet,
to those with many feet my love too.
Let the footless harm me not,
nor the two-footed do me harm,
let the four-footed harm me not,
nor the many-footed do me harm.
All creatures and all breathing things,
all beings none excepted,
good fortune may they see
and may no harm come near.
Infinite the Buddha!
Infinite the Dhamma!
Infinite the Sangha!
But finite are the creeping things -
snakes, scorpions and centipedes, spiders, lizards, rats.
Now I have made this warding and protection
So may those beings go away!
Him, I revere, the Blessed One.
Seven Samma-Sambuddhas I revere.

The Buddha recommended these verses on the occasion when a monk died of snakebite. It seems that they have proved effective ever since! The writer has heard of only one monk, a young American living by himself, no doubt with little or no training from a Teacher, who died from snakebite. On the other hand, monks who could not leave the jungle track they were on because of the steepness of the country even in the face of a herd of wild elephants, were not attacked as they sat meditating on loving-kindness.

The Buddha himself used loving-kindness when faced with the maddened bull elephant Nalagiri. His cousin, Devadatta, bribed the elephant-keepers to let this fierce creature out into the streets when the Buddha and the monks were on almsround. Seeing it charging down the street, trumpeting, red-eyed, ears spread out and tail rigid, everyone except the Buddha and his attendant, Venerable Ananda Thera, fled. The Buddha turned on to the tusker a ray of metta so powerful that the elephant lost all its aggressiveness and came and knelt down taking the dust from the Buddha's feet.

Another of jealous Devadatta's attempts to assassinate the Buddha involved groups or archers who were to shoot down the Buddha in the forest. The Buddha deliberately took the path where they were stationed and while walking focused his mind on metta. All of them dropped their weapons, begged his pardon and after listening to Dhamma became his devoted disciples. So strong can loving-kindness become!

Meditation Methods

Its power is also used for healing. Those who have such ability can heal others because of their own practice of metta - which could have been done in a past life. And those who wish to help others by healing should take up this practice now and so strengthen and purify their love for all beings.

This brings us to a brief consideration of the advantages of loving-kindness listed by the Buddha. First among the eleven benefits of establishing oneself in loving-kindness is: *one sleeps happily*, one goes to sleep with a wholesome subject - metta, which dissolves away all tensions. *One wakes happily*, not disgruntled, not drowsy, one gets up refreshed, happy and energetic. *One sees no evil dreams*, for none will afflict the person whose body, speech and mind are practising Dhamma and who has little conflict therefore. *One is dear to human beings*, not bringing about dissension wherever one goes, one brings only harmony and peace. *One is dear to non-humans*, meaning that ghosts and other invisible beings will not harm the meditator since he has protected himself with this excellent armour of loving-kindness. *The gods (devas) protect one*, for as the mind becomes calmer and more purified it comes to resemble those of the devas who, knowing this, will wish him well and protect the meditator from danger. *Neither fire nor poison nor weapons harm one*, for who would attack one who has made loving-kindness really strong? *One's mind is quickly concentrated*, because of an absence of strong defilements and because loving-kindness removes some obstructions due to past unwholesome kamma. *The expression on one's face is radiant*, one's face conveys the loving-kindness found in one's heart; also the meaning can be that one's complexion is radiant - without the expensive multitude of creams and lotions! *One dies unconfused*, no dullness or fear afflicts a person who's mind-heart is strongly established in metta at this time - a good mental subject which will ensure an excellent rebirth. *One attains to the Brahma-world if to nothing higher*, since even if one does not become a Noble One at the time of death, one is sure to arise in the realm of subtle form as a Brahma-god living there in excellent and purified states of mind. And if one knows the Dhamma one will then recollect that even the heavens of Brahma are impermanent and so feel impelled to continue with meditation practice until one of the Noble Paths and Fruits is reached.

It is notable that ten of the above eleven advantages are to be known *in this world*. Only one concerns the future life. This should be enough, surely, to attract even the most sceptical person who has no confidence in teachings on rebirth!

The practice of loving-kindness purifies the emotions, makes one truly a humane being, and is the mark of a true Buddhist. One cannot count oneself a follower of the Buddha who manifested such great loving-kindness and compassion for the world if one's anger is still unrestrained and one's heart still sullied with resentment. Even though one may know the Abhidhamma (voluminous works of Buddhist psychology) off backwards one does not count as a Buddhist until one behaves as one, with loving-kindness.

Those who choose to practise the Bodhisatta's path for the

eventual attainment of Buddhahood, have, in Theravada tradition, loving-kindness to practise as a perfection (*parami*), as a quality which carries one across the ocean of birth and earth with others as well. It is impossible to lead others to practise the Dhamma unless metta is strongly established in one's own heart. If others see one becoming angry or resentful will they not say to themselves, 'Well, he's the same as we are. What can we learn from him?' Only metta and the other practices of Dhamma can calm the wild waves of emotion so that one is cool inside when others are on fire.

All schools of Buddhist teaching advocate the practice of compassion, whether as an ordained follower or a lay person, whether striving on the path to Arahantship of Bodhisattahood. But there is no compassion in one who has not developed loving-kindness, for how can one have sympathy with others' sorrows if one's love has not grown beyond a narrow seeking for self-satisfaction? Without compassion, and so indifferent or callous, one can never really appreciate others' joy and so it is likely that one remains a prey to envy. And with no loving-kindness, compassion and joy-with-others, equanimity is sure to be absent so that one is at the mercy of the untamed stallions of the passions pulling one this way and that. The Buddha frequently praised the cultivation of these four qualities, calling them the Divine Abidings, the most excellent states leading to deliverance of the heart - but unless metta is cultivated the others do not come to fruition.

Here is the Buddha's eulogy of loving-kindness to close this section.

> Monks, whatever kinds of worldly merit there are, all are not worth one sixteenth part of the heart-deliverance of loving-kindness; in shining and beaming and radiance the heart-deliverance of loving-kindness far excels them. Just as whatever light there is of stars, all is not worth one sixteenth part of the moon's light... and just as in the last month of the Rains, in the Autumn when the heavens are clear, the sun as he climbs the heavens drives all darkness from the sky with his shining and beaming and radiance; as just as when the night is turning to dawn, the Morning Star is shining and beaming and radiating; so too, whatever kinds of worldly merit there are, all are not worth one sixteenth part of the heart-deliverance of loving-kindness...[16]

2. Mindfulness of Breathing (Ānapānasati):

This meditation subject was, by tradition, used by Gotama in his efforts to attain Enlightenment. It is most suitable for promoting calm and concentrated states and so for quelling the distracted mind. It is taught in a number of different ways but in all of them the meditator must first find one point in the concentration process where the breath can be watched. Concentration upon the touch of the breath as it enters and leaves the nostrils is the place most often taught. But this is not suitable for people who have much tension in the head and neck, nor for those whose minds find mindfulness of the

Meditation Methods

breath's contact too subtle. In both cases it is better to watch the rising and falling of the diaphragm which is far from the centre of tension and a grosser and therefore more easily observed place.

The aim in any case should be a steady watchfulness so that the beginning of the in-breath, its end, the pause if any, and the out-breath's beginning and end, are all clearly known, one is aware of all stages of the breathing process. There are a number of supports for intensifying mindfulness of breathing, such as taking note of the length of the in and out breaths, noting one as 'long' and another as 'short'. Another method often taught is counting the breaths, saying to oneself 'one' on the in-breath, 'one' on the outbreath, counting only up to ten. If thoughts arise before ten breaths have passed - and beginners find it remarkable to experience three breaths without distraction! - then begin again at 'one' as soon as mindfulness has detected the deviation. One should not count beyond ten as then it is easy for the mind to get lost and unmindful of breathing. After ten mindful breaths go back to 'one'. This method may be used until strong calm is reached when the counting can be discontinued.

Other Teachers train their disciples to repeat a word like 'Buddho' or 'Arahang' - both meaning Enlightened One, or 'Dhammo' (the Truth, Teaching) 'Sangho' (the community of those enlightened by practising Dhamma), in time with the breath. Thus 'Bud' is repeated on the in-breath and 'dho' on the out-breath until calm is attained. When this occurs either the repetition which is really the Recollection of the Buddha's qualities, or else the subtle breathing, may be followed as one's meditation subject. Advice on such choices is usually given by Teachers to their pupils but where people practise alone they have to decide which subject suits them best.

The mindful stages of this practice have already been outlined in the last chapter and so need not be repeated here. There remains to be described only some way to judge how successful the practice is. One must bear in mind what has been said already in the section on loving-kindness, specially that defilements in everyday life should be less troublesome while relations with others should become easier. If it is otherwise something is wrong!

One may evaluate success in this way: If the mind is continuously fixed on 'breathing-in-out' with no attention paid to other sense-objects, not even other parts of the body, and no discursive thought, then one is doing well. If one does perceive other sense-objects, for instance, loud or soft noises from outside but one's mind is not shaken from the concentration on breathing-in-out, merely having awareness of these things which returns immediately to the breathing when they cease, without discursive thought, then concentration is good. If the mind is mostly fixed on breathing-in-out but also strays to body (touch) consciousness in other parts of the body but is still without discursiveness, then it is not so bad. But if one's breathing-in-out-mind is frequently disturbed by other mental states consisting of ideas, pictures etc. then there is still a lot of work to do. And even if one's meditation is up to the first standard, there is no need for complacency as much more can still be done.

When calm is being cultivated with this method the tranquil flow of the breath is most important but if mindfulness is turned to the development of insight then the arising and passing away aspect of the breath should be regarded. When arising and passing of the breaths are noticed continually over a longer or shorter period, according to a person's development, then impermanence becomes clear, or else the disturbance inherent in the bodily process of breathing becomes noticeable - this means seeing subtle dukkha, or again, awareness comes that there is no person who is breathing, only a breath process, which insight, if complete is the penetration of not self and attainment of Arahantship. But insight into the impermanence, for instance, of the breaths will not arise until there is strong calm - it is the impermanence of that calm that has to be seen. Neither impermanence nor the other two characteristics can be discerned by the scattered and distracted mind.

3. *Walking Meditation (Cankamana)*:

This type of meditation aims primarily at insight but by means of it quite a lot of calm may be developed. It is especially suitable for those of a vigorous active nature and it can be a medicine too for those who incline to lethargy and drowsiness.

The requirements for this practice are a place to walk back and forth twenty or more paces long, preferably quiet and secluded. The walk should not be shorter than twenty paces because when one is always turning round the mind may become too easily confused. It may be longer however, specially if one has a good stride and clear concentration. The meditation-walks of some Teachers in Thailand are as much as even sixty paces long. This will be too much for a beginner whose mind may even stray within twenty paces.

When a meditation-walk is constructed in a forest or elsewhere in the country there is no difficulty about seclusion. One can choose a place which is quiet and easily make it according to tradition. It is usually surfaced with fine sand where one can practise on it barefoot, otherwise any level material may be used. Besides being level it should be straight and if it will be used during the day some shade or shelter may be required. In Thailand and other tropical countries these paths are always within a thicket of trees so that they are comparatively cool. Also, it is customary to construct the path east-west rather than north-south though the writer does not know the reason for this. A useful feature of many meditation-walks is a seat of bricks or stone at one end on which the meditator can sit cross-legged when enough walking has been done.

In towns a quiet part of one's garden or even a passage inside a building where one will not be disturbed will be quite suitable. If the length is restricted it is better to walk slowly while more space gives a chance to walk at normal speeds. In fact the normal speed of walking is preferable to some methods which teach ultra-slow movement. The reason is that mindfulness is actually to be applied in everyday life and not only for special meditation courses. One must be mindful at one's usual speed and in normal situations! But fast walking can be useful to stir up energy when tiredness is blanketing the mind, also when one feels vigorous. The speed of walking will tend to slow down with greater concentration until that particular way of walking which is both relaxed and alert becomes a natural feature of oneself.

Before beginning the practice stand silently at the end of the walk and review what one is doing it for. Those who have confidence in the Triple Gem raise their hands together in reverence remembering that the Buddha has praised the meditation-walk as having five benefits: it hardens one for travelling, promotes vigorous effort, helps digestion after meals, is healthy, and the concentration won upon the walk lasts a long time. Then lower the hands, clasp them in front right over left and begin walking with the right foot.

If thoughts afflict the mind midway between the ends, stop until they have gone. At each end, check the mind while stopping momentarily before setting off down the walk again. And of course, do not let the eyes roam here and there; they should be focused upon the earth or floor and kept there.

How long one walks for must depend on time available and the amount of practice one likes to do. In north-east Thailand where there are good meditation Teachers, villagers spend a whole day in the local Wat (monastery-temple) up to four times a month. The night-time is particularly stressed as suitable for intensive meditation and some of those people show that they make the best use of their opportunities. In the morning deep tracks can be seen worn into the sand of the Wat area where for hours on end they have done the meditation-walk, perhaps alternating it with sitting practice. Monks and novices too may practise the meditation walk for long periods of time through the night. It is effective at quelling lethargy and drowsiness though of course some physical tiredness must be expected. Great efforts produce great results! Of course, they do not have to be physical ones and effort equally great may be made by the meditator who has resolved to sit through the night – but such efforts leave no traces in the sand and so cannot be known easily.

What should one be mindful of during walking meditation? This varies with different people, some notice the contact of the feet on the earth, others the movements of the legs, and so on. At first just be generally mindful of the whole walking process, later the mind will single out something interesting which should be investigated.

When the mind has become quite calm and stays 'at home' not going anywhere, then start the development of insight by viewing the walking in the light of impermanence, or dukkha, or not self, according to which mode of investigation comes easily. In the walking-process too, as with breathing, there is an illustration of impermanence, of arising and passing, beginning and ending. That should be looked into until all the mind attends only to it. Dukkha can be seen there too, some physical pain maybe as well as the subtle dukkha of changefulness. And then there is not self: Who walks? Who walks?

This form of meditation is used to the exclusion of any others by some people and it is suitable for leading them even to the fruits of

Enlightenment, as Arahants, as the following story shows:

> After reciting the monastic rule on the Full Moon day (at Situlpava in southern Sri Lanka), one of two brothers who were senior monks went to his own dwelling-place surrounded by the community of monks. As he stood on the walk looking at the moonlight he calculated his own lifespan, and he said to the community of monks 'In what way have you seen monks attaining Nibbana up till now?' Some answered 'Till now we have seen them attain Nibbana sitting in their seats'. Others answered 'We have seen them sitting crosslegged in the air'. The senior monk said 'I shall now show you one attaining Nibbana while walking.' He then drew a line on the walk, saying, 'I shall go from this end of the walk to the other end and return; when I reach this line I shall attain Nibbana'. So saying he stepped on to the walk and went to the far end. On his return he attained Nibbana in the same moment in which he stepped on the line.[17]

4. Perception of the Unattractive (asubha-saññā):

Just as loving-kindness is the medicine for the aversion-sickness, so this meditation cures the disease of lust and greed. Unlike the practice of loving-kindness it is not very popular, as people wish to be rid of aversion because of its painfulness but are not so keen to lay greed aside since it seems so much bound up with pleasure. But for the person in whom the root of greed is strong and who sees clearly the dukkha which it brings with it, including of course aversion when expectations are disappointed, this meditation-subject will be a welcome cure. And in to-day's world where one is constantly tempted to go all out for pleasures and possessions, where there is such a mighty array of diversifying possibilities, and where the root of greed is therefore constantly titillated, this subject is much needed.

There are two ways of practising it. The first of them may be briefly mentioned as the original method of practising is no longer possible. In the days of the Buddha corpses were often disposed of by taking them to a special area of forest or mountain and there letting them decompose, both elements and animals helping the process. Such a 'bone-yard' was used by various religious wanderers and monks who realized that the objects to be seen there stimulated renunciation. Buddhist monks too visited such places and contemplated the various stages of decay of the body. An elaborate description of what should be done when one goes there is contained in *The Path of Purification*, Chapter Six, written about one thousand years after the Buddha but based upon much earlier commentaries. And such a tradition has continued down to the present day in Buddhist lands though bodies there are usually cremated and never in these days left to decay.

What happened in the Buddha's days can be illustrated by the story of Sirima, a famous courtesan then. She had confidence in the Buddha's teachings and gave choice almsfood to eight monks every day. One young monk hearing of her beauty resolved to go and see her by collecting one of the eight tickets she sent to the monastery. The day he went however, she was ill and could not serve the monks herself but had to be carried in by the girls in her house. Even when sick her beauty inflamed the young monk's desire and he fell deeply in love with her. Returning to the monastery he could think of nothing else except Sirimā, refusing even to eat and get up for four days running. The evening of the day when she became ill, Sirimā died. The king sent a message to the Buddha telling him, as she was one of his followers. The Buddha asked the king to have the body guarded for a few days in the 'bone-yard'. This was done and after four days the Buddha announced his intention of going to view the body accompanied by his monks and nuns. The king commanded that all citizens should attend with the exception of caretakers. All went out to the bone-yard and stood each group in their own places, around the bloated corpse of Sirimā. That young monk too, hearing that the Buddha would visit Sirimā, went along overjoyed. When all assembled the king instructed the town criers to announce that Sirima's body would be put up for sale. In her life men had paid a thousand coins a night for her company, but as she was now dead, the king instructed the criers first to set a price of half this amount. There were no takers. And though the king brought the price down by halving it each time, until the corpse was offered free, there were no takers at all. The Buddha then uttered the following verse:-

> See this body beautiful,
> a mass of sores, a congeries,
> much considered but miserable
> where nothing is stable, nothing persists -

and that young monk became a stream-winner while many others were established in the Dhamma.[18]

However, the Buddha's emphasis was not so much upon seeing others' bodies decay but seeing that one's own will do so. Hence in his Discourse on the Foundations of Mindfulness he says: 'Again, a monk judges this same body *as though* he were looking at a corpse thrown on a charnel ground, one-day dead, two-days dead, three-days dead, bloated, livid and oozing with matter (thinking): "This body too is of such a nature, will become like that, and has not escaped from that"'! It is this most highly prized body, the object of so much greed, lust and attachment, which has to be seen as a bloated corpse, or one which is gnawed or dismembered, or which has been reduced to a skeleton with tendons, or to scattered bones, or even to bones crumbling into dust. Visualizing one's body in any of these ways can be very effective indeed in ridding the heart of lust, especially if one has a visual type of mind. But great care is needed if one practises this meditation without a Teacher's guidance. There is nothing dangerous in the meditation itself but one's own reactions, meaning what the defilements do, could be rather uncontrollable. And if one visualizes one's body as decayed in some particular way again and again, eventually a vision may arise at the time of the mind entering the neighbourhood-concentration (see Chapter IV) of the body, in that condition. Then it is no longer a case of 'myself with a healthy body visualizing a corpse' but *one's body actually being perceived as a corpse*. If one is not mature through Dhamma-practice, or if one has a timid nature, then much suffering, even mental imbalance, could follow. Therefore it is not advisable to practise this method intensively or for long periods of time without someone who can give one guidance.

The second method known as perception of unattractiveness analyses one's own body and dissipates lust by discovering only unpleasant bodily organs and substances. The body when young and well can be attractive as a whole, when perceived, as the Pali expression has it, 'all-of-a-lump', but even bodies which are in the bloom of youth and good health fail to excite attachment when regarded in the light of their constituent parts.

A warning here. This meditation is not for analysing others' bodies into unattractive collections of bits and pieces, it is for seeing one's own in this way. If others, maybe those of the opposite sex, are regarded in this way, aversion towards them may be aroused. Others should be treated with loving-kindness as far as possible, while one's own greed and lust will be dissolved by seeing one's own body in this analytical way. And of course the aim is not to arouse hatred for one's own body either but just to still greed. If self-hatred arises through practising this meditaiton then a change is needed; more time should be spent on developing loving-kindness towards oneself.

The Buddha's words describing this meditation are as follows: 'This very body, from the soles of the feet up, from the crown of the head down, surrounded by skin, is full of various mean impurities. There are in this body: hair of the head, hair of the body, nails, teeth, skin, flesh, sinews, bones, bone-marrow, kidneys, heart, liver, membranes, spleen, lungs, large gut, small gut, gorge, dung, bile, phlegm, pus, blood, sweat, fat, tears, skin-grease, spittle, snot, oil of the joints, urine.' Apart from this passage he gives no special way of meditating on the body. Later commentators however, have suggested a way of practice which involves dividing the list into groups and then going forwards and backwards through these items concentrating on each one in turn. This is perhaps too diffuse for most people as it offers too many chances for the mind to wander. It is better just to take a few of these parts and go through them. The first five, for instance, are told to every Buddhist novice and monk during their ordination as a meditation to combat lust whenever it arises. These five include everything that we see of a person; put together by the mind they may be attractive but individually they have nothing inherently beautiful about them.

It is important here to realize that the Buddha has no aversion to beauty as such (for this would be just frustrated desire - which can be seen in many ascetics). He himself was outstandingly handsome and so were many of his monk and nun disciples. The trouble does not lie in beauty but rather in the attachment which people have for it.[19] Hence, beauty, that is the body, is not to be punished with 'disciplines' or mortified with severe austerities but rather the mind,

Meditation Methods

where attachment lies, is to be trained to look at the other side of the body's beauty, its unattractive aspect.

The body, 'all of a lump' can be seen as beautiful but that disappears when the parts composing it are considered. By themselves, head hair, body hair, nails, teeth and skin have nothing of beauty. Still less are the internal organs of the body beautiful. The outsides of bodies may be attractive but what attachment is possible for 'flesh, sinews, bones, bone-marrow' and so on? No one wants to see these things yet they are all parts of what I call myself, and they are necessary in all the bodies to which we become attached. How easy it is not to remember this!

One may choose those first five parts and then concentrate on each in turn. Do not aim to see them as foul or disgusting, for this will only be inverted desire which is, of course, aversion. Just observe each one mentally with the minimum of discursiveness either regarding each part silently, or if concentration is not strong enough for this then repeating the name of each part to oneself. The unattractive aspect of each part will then become obvious quite naturally.

Some people may find it more effective to use a selection of items from the list above, such as, 'blood, flesh, bones' or 'large gut, small gut, gorge, dung' - one should choose those parts which are unattractive to oneself.

Others may find it better to use just one part - 'bones' is often used, and even then to limit concentration to some particular area of the body's bones. The important thing in any case is to gain a quiet mind through this practice where the subject of meditation is continuously present. When dwelt on for long the result can be liberation of the mind by wisdom as shown in the following story:-

> It seems that as the Elder (Mahātissa) was on his way from Cetiyapabbata to Anuradhapura (in northern Sri Lanka) for alms, a certain daughter-in-law of a clan, who had quarrelled with her husband and had set out early from Anurādhapura all dressed up and tricked out like a celestial nymph to go to her relatives' home, saw him on the road, and being low-minded, she laughed a loud laugh. (Wondering) 'What is that?' the Elder looked up and finding in the bones of her teech the perception of unattractiveness, he attained Arahantship. But her husband who was going after her saw the Elder and asked 'Venerable sir, did you by chance see a woman?' The Elder told him:
>
> > Whether it was a man or woman
> > that went by I noticed not;
> > but only that on this high road
> > there goes a group of bones.[20]

Care is required with this second practice of the body's unattractiveness and much of what was said above applies here too. An additional consideration for both of these practices is that if one has a partner with whom there are sexual relations, that person should be considered before doing much of this practice. It does cut down sexual desire in oneself and if there is not to be trouble, the other person's happiness has to be considered.

5. *Recollection of the Buddha (Buddhānussati):*

This is a meditation very suitable for people having strong confidence in the Buddha as their Teacher, but who are rather weak in concentration. It is good too for those with the sort of mind that visualizes easily.

In case one has a visual mind where a picture can be held fairly steady then the recollection of a particularly beautiful Buddha-image can be very inspiring and fruitful for the development of calm. Hold that Buddha-image steady, returning to it each time mindfulness slips. Contemplation of a picture like this has already gone beyond the use of words and so represents a more purified state than the mind which has to rely on them. The picture however, should be as simple as possible - one should not tire out the mind by trying to recollect complicated decorations. Just the form of the Buddha should be taken.

But if words have to be used then the Sutta passage which is the basis of this practice is as follows: 'Indeed the Blessed One is thus: the accomplished destroyer of defilements, a Buddha perfected by himself, complete in clear knowledge and compassionate conduct, supremely good in presence and in destiny, knower of the worlds, incomparable master of men to be tamed, teacher of devas and men, awakened and awakener, and the lord by skilful means apportioning Dhamma.'

The whole passage may be repeated dwelling on each of the nine qualities of the Buddha in turn, either in English or in Pali (Iti pi so Bhagavā...) In the latter case the meaning of each of these qualities will be known but if repeated in English some explanation of them is needed. Here is a summary of the most important points.[21]

The accomplished destroyer of defilements (arahaṁ): means that the Buddha was completely free of all trace of greed, aversion and delusion. He had a purity which did not need to be maintained by mindfulness but which was natural to one in whom there is no longer any conflict. He was supremely worthy, therefore, to accept gifts from others - they gave to a man purified of all passion, cooled down, with no fires burning - one who could teach them how to attain a similar state or help them out of worldly difficulties, according to their desires.

A Buddha perfected by himself (sammā-sambuddho): Not only had he purified the mind-heart of all defilements, he discovered the way to do this by himself. He had no teacher who showed him how this should be done, he investigated into his own heart and found there the way of Dhamma. Having done so he awakened to the truth and taught the way. The truth to be discovered is the Four Noble Truths and the way to be enlightened regarding them is the way of mindfulness.

Complete in clear knowledge and compassionate conduct

Meditation Methods

(vijjācaraṇa-sampanno): Some know a lot but their conduct is not in accordance with their knowledge. Others' conduct is good but they have no penetrative wisdom. The Buddha combined these two perfectly, his purity and great compassion expressed as conduct was always rooted in wisdom. His conduct could never be criticized by the wise as it was always naturally pure, his wisdom was always appropriate for the persons and situations he encountered.

Supremely good in presence and in destiny (sugato): This paraphrase is needed to bring out the meaning of *Sugato* (lit. 'well-gone'). His going was always good, for wherever he went it was for the benefit and happiness of the people there. And at the end of his life, his Great Nibbana was good too, for his 'going' (not going to any place, as the fire which *goes out* does not go anywhere) was completion of what he had discovered forty-five years earlier, at the time of his Awakening.

Knower of the worlds (lokavidū): all kinds of worlds were known by him, first, other planets, solar systems and galaxies, second, the different worlds of rebirth; and third, the 'world' of the mind with all its intricacies. He knew them through the insight that arose when he discovered Awakening and saw the Dhamma which is true in all worlds everywhere.

Incomparable master of men to be tamed (anuttaro-purisadammasārathi): He was able to tame very powerful and troublesome people because he knew just how their minds worked and exactly what method was required to tame them, beginning always with a gentle approach and only using severity occasionally. He trained people without any recourse to physical violence though occasionally using shock techniques in his teaching, and more rarely employing feats of supernormal success. Angulimala's story, of the bandit who wore a garland of his victims' fingers, illustrates both these things. Of his Master, the Buddha, Angulimala had this to say:-

> There are some that tame with beatings,
> Some with goads and some with lashes;
> One has neither rod nor weapon -
> I am tamed by such as he'[22]

Teacher of devas and men (satthā-deva-manussānaṁ): Generally the Teacher taught Dhamma to human beings in the daytime; to lay people when he was invited to their houses in the morning and when they went to the grove where he stayed in the afternoon. The evening was the time when he taught monks and nuns. The devas, divinities or gods, were taught by him during the quietest part of the night, usually in the small hours of the morning well before dawn.

Awakened and Awakener (buddho): He had no need to teach Dhamma after experiencing Awakening. He did not want to have disciples and he had no desire to convert the world, indeed he had no desires at all. But many beings were attracted to him and out of Great Compassion for their dukkha he taught them the way to Awaken themselves.

And the Lord by skilful means apportioning Dhamma (bhagavā), for he was able to analyse the Dhamma in the ways necessary for helping beings. He could select just the right Dhamma for everyone who came to him, just as a good doctor can choose the right medicine for his patients.

Such a method of meditation must begin by being rather discursive. If too much wandering of the mind sets in while practising it then it will be better to shorten it, using just a few of the nine epithets and selecting those that give the deepest response from one's heart. These should then be repeated in the same way as the whole list with pauses for reflection.

When even this amount of latitude brings distraction only one epithet should be chosen and this one should repeat in rythm with the breath - such as 'Bud - dho'. No time should be allowed for reflection, instead the repetition of the Buddha's quality which has been chosen should be continued throughout the meditation period. Preferably, an effort should be made too, to keep it going during one's work, or if that is not possible, during such periods of the day when close concentration is not necessary. Under the section on Daily Mindfulness (Chapter II.3) some of these times have been suggested. Instead of bare attention being applied then one could take up the repetition of one of the Buddha's epithets.

The Buddha himself praised those people who became established in the 'four here-and-now-seen-abidings-in-bliss of the well-developed mind', that is, being firmly confident in each of the Three Jewels, the Buddha, Dhamma and Sangha, plus protecting one's precepts so that virtue is 'complete and perfect, spotless and pure, conducive to liberation, praised by the wise, something to which one is not attached and which is favourable to concentration'. So this recollection of the Buddha is the first of these which anyone may practise with benefit and so deepen confidence in the Buddha as their Teacher.

A remarkable case of one who hardly had to practise but for whom just one glance at the Buddha was enough for his heart to be established in serene confidence, is the story of 'Burnished Earrings', a millionaire miser's son. This millionaire, nicknamed 'Never-gave' was reluctant to call a doctor when his son went down with jaundice. Going to a doctor at last he asked him what would be suitable for such and such symptoms and remembered the doctor's reply. But even though he dosed his son with the remedy he had concocted, Burnished Earrings got no better. Finally he had the youth carried out on to the verandah so that people coming to commiserate at his death would not see the accumulated wealth. The Buddha through his compassionate net of knowledge which he spread early each morning in meditation came to know that the young man would place confidence in him and so die serene. On almsround with other monks he passed the miser's house and managed to attract the young man's attention. Though he was so weak that he could not raise his hands in respectful greeting yet his heart was full of confidence in the Buddha and on dying soon after, was reborn as a deva with great splendour.

Though for us in the later age this recollection centres in the beginning on Gotama the Buddha's qualities, truly these are the marks of all Perfectly Enlightened Ones. Gradually as concentration deepens and some insight occurs, this recollection will lead to what is Buddha in one's own heart. And then one will begin to know what *Buddhaṁ saraṅam gacchāmi* - To the Buddha I go for refuge - really means.

NOTES TO CHAPTER V

[1] See *The Path of Purification*, Chs.IV-IX for them.
[2] All quoted from *The Path of Purification* trans. by Bhikkhu Nyanamoli (B.P.S., Kandy), p. 324.
[3] The whole Discourse should be read and earnestly reflected on. See *The Practice of Loving-Kindness*, Wheel No. 7 (B.P.S., Kandy).
[4] Author's translation of Dhammapada verses 252-253.
[5] This refers to a monk's or nun's going forth to Homelessness.
[6] See below (H) 'Who are you angry with?'
[7] Dhammapada 125.
[8] Jātaka No. 313. See Jataka Stories Vols. III-IV, p. 26.
[9] The order of these factors is according to the translation used, not always the same as the Pali original. See below for the full translation.
[10] Dhammapada verse 134.
[11] *The Practice of Loving-kindness*, Wheel No. 7 (B.P.S., Kandy).
[12] An inspiring account be read in, *The Life of Phra Acharn Mun, Meditation Master*.
[13] *Anguttara Nikaya, an Anthology*, Wheel No. 155-158 (B.P.S., Kandy).
[14] *The Path of Purification*, Ch. IX. p. 323.
[15] It is not certain what snakes are meant by those four names but for English recitation one might change to: My love to the lordly cobras, and to the pythons my love too, my love to the vipers, adders, and to the black Gotamas too...
[16] *The Practice of Loving-Kindness*, Wheel No. 7 (B.P.S., Kandy).
[17] *The Path of Purification* (B.P.S., Kandy), Ch. VIII, para. 244.
[18] For the full story see *Dhammapada Stories* Vol. II. (B.P.S., Kandy).
[19] The expression in English 'lusts of the flesh', or even 'bodily desire', is quite misleading as the body has no desires at all, only the mind.
[20] *The Path of Purification*, Ch. 1. para. 55, (B.P.S., Kandy). And see *Bag of Bones, a Miscellany on the Body*, same publishers.
[21] For incidents in the Buddha's Life which illustrate these qualities, see Ch. XII in *The Splendour of Enlightenment* (A Life of the Buddha), Mahamakut Press, Bangkok, 1979.
[22] Discourse on Angulimala, No. 86 of Majjhima-nikāya. Translated by Ven. Nyanamoli in *A Treasury of the Buddha's Discourses*, (B.P.S., Kandy).

And One's Heart well Purifying

VI

GOOD RESULTS AND BAD

We live in an achievement-oriented society. Good results are looked on as the natural result of hard work. Well, no work is harder than meditation! Perhaps we think the results must be good and come quickly? And if they don't maybe this proves that meditation is a waste of time! Look round for another trip!

Quite often people do not experience the results they look for. Suppose a person thinks that profound meditation is signalled by lights and visions - which a friend has told him all about - and these things do not happen, does that mean he is getting nothing for his efforts? Remember, there are always results from making kamma; even trying to meditate a little every day is good kamma and will produce the results of happiness. But those results may not be obvious immediately. Sometimes a meditator may have made unwholesome kamma in the past and this now prevents the immediate fruiting of new good kamma. In other words, the ease of concentration, bliss, peace and insight may be blocked for some time. The only thing to do then is to go on! Those who give up at this point, saying, 'Oh, I don't get anything from it!' are like people who set out to do a long walk but turn back after the first mile. They never get to see anything!

So if your meditation produces no spectacular results, just carry on. It is better actually if there are no such results because such things can be snares and traps.

Progress should be measured by results in everyday life. Can you bear Mr. Brown now? Have you more patience with Mrs. Smith? Less temper and more loving-kindness, less resentment and more happiness? Can you see things more clearly, more in the light of Dhamma than formerly? Do you have more equanimity and not get upset so often? These are good results from practising meditation regularly.

Some people though deceive themselves. They feel that as they meditate everyday they are becoming truly spiritual. In their anxiety to see their own purity they manage to overlook glaring faults, as the story of Loving-kindness and the Tea-tray makes clear. It seems that there was a man in Sri Lanka who meditated on his bed for half an hour every morning after rising. He pervaded the whole world with loving-kindness in the ten directions going through all the combinations of creatures. At the end of this time his servant brought him 'bed-tea' - a tray with tea-pot, hot water, cup, milk and sugar. On this particular day the man had suffused the whole world, nay the universe, with metta and then a tap on his door indicated that the tea had arrived. As usual he called out 'Come in' and his servant entered but on this occasion tripped on a corner of carpet and lost his balance. The tea, water, sugar and milk with broken crockery and an apologetic servant were strewn all over the floor. The all-pervading metta-meditator exclaimed 'What are you doing, you fool! Can't you see I'm practising loving-kindness!'

One's blind spots may not be as bad as this but still meditation should have the result of increasing understanding and self-restraint.

In the example above the deluded man also suffered from conceit, the bane of people who practise regularly. As this can be counted a real danger it is dealt with more fully in the next chapter.

'Traps and snares' were mentioned already, especially visions. It is easy for the inexperienced meditator to become attached to visions, especially where these are beautiful. For instance, a beginner in meditation once sat on a meditation retreat for two or three days and watched an endless panorama of landscapes all in very beautiful muted colours float by - as though unwound from a scroll-painting. He was advised to place his attention elsewhere! Some meditators not only see pleasant and beautiful things but behold religious symbols which they take to be a 'revelation'. This is just becoming attached to the products of one's own mind! That visions of this sort are usually the mind's products is proved by the fact that for instance, Catholics see Christ or the Virgin Mary but never Krishna; while devotees of the latter may see him sporting in the Himalayan regions but never behold the Prophet riding from Medina to Mecca! Similarly among Buddhists: those of Theravada persuasion are rather unlikely to behold Kwan Yin though they may see the Buddha-to-be, the Bodhisatta Ariya Metteyya in his bejewelled abode on the plane of the Tusita Heaven. Meditators and mystics the world over are too much given to believing in the machinations of their own minds.

A Buddhist therefore, who sees a vision of a Buddha does not, unless he is heavily deluded, imagine that he has seen Gotama or some other Buddha! Seeing Buddhas, even when visualization is part of meditation practice, does not necessarily purify the heart of defilements. How easy it would be for people with visual minds if this happened! Visualization techniques are therefore only of benefit when the visions actually bring increasing purity in mind, speech and body actions (kam_mas). If they lead to conceit, ('I can merge myself with Maitreya...Tarā... 'etc.), the meditator badly needs some advice!

A typical Buddhist attitude to visions is brought out in the following incident which happened a few years ago. A monk in Thailand sat down to meditate as he usually did for an hour or so in the afternoon. This time though it seemed that he travelled down a long dark tunnel and found at the end someone who took him on a tour, guiding him with his hand. The monk never saw the rest of this person, only the hand on his arm, and heard a voice explain the various bloody and horrific tortures which he saw. This was a vision of a hell-realm. The voice explained what different kammas had brought on the various forms of intense suffering. The tour was long, the place immense and the monk emerged from his experience only when the dark night sky was full of stars. He had sat for many hours, far longer than he had ever been able to do. When he told his Teacher about it his comment was, 'Why didn't you find out *who* took you on the tour?' Had he done so, instead of permitting the mind to ramble on and be fascinated, he might have investigated who was producing it all.

A more amusing tale though rather dangerous, was that of the monk who saw at the other end of his meditation-walk, a brilliant and sublimely beautiful light. He walked towards it, and as he did so, it rose up a tree-trunk. He climbed the tree - and it appeared at the end of a branch. He crawled to the end of the branch, at which it hopped twenty feet or so to the next tree. Fortunately for him, at this point his mindfulness returned! He realized that he was indulging in wrong concentration, and perhaps that something else which did not wish him well was trying to harm him.

Rather more violent a story and considerably older, is the incident of the Zen Master's advice to a very pious monk who indulged in visions: 'When you see the Buddha, kill him!' Though one cannot imagine such words being spoken by a Theravada Teacher still the teaching is characteristically Buddhist.

Great Teachers in Thailand stress that visions may be either the product of one's own mind or external realities. As an example: one meditator seeing a vision of devas would be letting subconscious memories well up to produce an image from the store of sense-impressions retained there. There are pictures of devas, usually saluting the Buddha, in almost every temple in Thailand. But another person might actually see devas, that is beings apart from himself and communicate with them. Teachers emphasize that it is very difficult for most meditators even those who have done much practice, to distinguish between these two types of experience. And of course the danger is that one becomes attached to visions whether their source is in one's own mind, or exterior. Conceit too raises its ugly head among people who have had 'experiences' like this. How full of their 'experiences' they are and how they eagerly relate them to others, again and again! Alas, instead of meditating to cut off the defilements, of which conceit is the root, they just strengthen them!

The only useful visions are those which can be made into 'work-places' (kammaṭṭhāna), that is, the sort that can be used as the meditation-subject. These are all visions of the body's messy bits and pieces, or of its death and decay. Such visions do not trap meditators into attachment, though working with them is not for those with timid minds. They can lead all the way to insight and liberation.

Fear can easily arise with these last sort of visions, such strong fear that a meditator could give up practising or even lose mindfulness for some time so that others would describe him as mentally unbalanced. This can also occur if during very peaceful meditation the breathing process stops. Then panic can be the result and the thought arises, 'I am dying'. Instead of letting go at this point, as one should - for one will not die even though no longer breathing, one hastily grasps at the familiar breath. Such an experience could also induce a meditator to give up practice.

Fear of these things and fears of more external causes for life ending, such as snakes, tigers and so on, come up more readily when one stays in the wilds, especially in caves or at the foot of a tree when the body has no protection against wild animals. Then the mind starts playing tricks and telling one that tigers, snakes, demons or ghosts are creeping up and about to cause one's death! The Bodhisatta, before his Enlightenment, also experienced such fears. As the Buddha, he later described his fears and the way he overcame them. Having gone to stay in specially remote places where various spirits were reported to dwell, at night, '...while I dwelt there, a wild animal would come up to me, or a peacock would knock off a branch, or the wind would rustle the leaves. I thought "Why do I dwell always expecting fear and dread? What if I subdue that fear and dread while keeping the posture that I am in when it finds me?"[1] After that, every time that fear arose he subdued it in that posture, for instance, if he was sitting then he would subdue it while sitting and not get up until it has vanished.

This is the way for those with very strong effort and mindfulness but another will be suggested below for meditators needing more support.

Similar accounts of intense fear are found among the accounts of Ven. Meditation Master Mun and his disciples in north-east Thailand. A particularly vivid incident is that of the monk who was afraid of ghosts (and by implication, of corpses and burning grounds). He was driven nearly mad by his own fears which however, he steeled himself to face courageously. Neither the lonely forest, nor the burning corpse, nor the sounds of an approaching 'ghost' - which turned out to be a half-starved village dog scavenging, caused him to flee. This is an example of conquest of fear. In the book that it is taken from there are several other remarkable cases of this too.

As in the case of the Bodhisatta, these are accounts of people who can stand hardship and solitude but what about ordinary folk who experience fear but wish to go on with their practice? The Buddha recommended, in his Discourse called 'The Foremost Flag', three things to cure 'fear, trembling and the hair standing on end'. These are the passages on recollection of the Buddha, Dhamma and Sangha which when recited to oneself in a moment of intense fear can give one heart as the banner of a great king in battle may give courage to his troops. These passages are given in full here and may be learnt by heart so that they come to mind readily whenever they are needed. They are usually recited by Buddhists every day.

> Indeed the Blessed One is thus: the Accomplished destroyer of defilements, a Buddha perfected by himself, complete in clear knowledge and compassionate conduct, Supremely good in presence and in destiny, Knower of the worlds, Imcomparable Master of men to be tamed, Teacher of devas and men, Awakened and awakener, and the Lord by skilful means apportioning Dhamma.
>
> The Dhamma of the Blessed One is perfectly expounded, to be seen here and now, not delayed in time, inviting one to come and see, leading inwards, to be known by the wise each for himself.
>
> The Sangha of the Blessed One's disciples has entered on the Good Way; the Sangha of the Blessed One's disciples has entered

on the Straight Way; The Sangha of the Blessed One's disciples has entered on the True Way; the Sangha of the Blessed One's disciples has entered on the Proper Way; that is to say - the four pairs of men, the eight types of persons[2] - this Sangha of the Blessed One's disciples is fit for gifts, fit for hospitality, fit for offerings and fit for reverential salutation, as the incomparable field of merits for the world.

The Buddha guarantees that 'fear, trembling and the hair standing on end' will vanish after one or more of these passages have been recited mindfully while dwelling on the meaning.

Some other bad results of meditation are the strengthening of views and narrow intolerance. These can go along together as they are typical of the 'conceit-and-views' complex. Views have already been explained (Chapter IV.3). Grasping at them is one of the forms of grasping to be abandoned through insight. But before people get to this, or because the teaching they follow lacks an insight-tradition, their regular meditation practice can make them very rigid in their ideas. The mind incorporating the idea of self, always seeks for things which can be grasped at for stability. Meditation when it succeeds to some extent, can strengthen the self-soul idea - and not lead necessarily to such good results as increased loving-kindness and compassion.

This danger can accompany intolerance:- 'Only my guru is right!' 'Only my line of teachers is right!' Such attitudes, which can only produce conflict, are just more subtle ways of saying, 'I AM RIGHT!' The old self-soul-ego has its say, even among Buddhists! If meditation is used for this purpose then it is going exactly opposite to the direction of Dhamma. Conceit is the most dangerous defilement for the meditator and in the next chapter it will be analysed in some detail.

Another undesirable result of meditation comes from using a subject not suited to one's character. And here the isolated meditator is in difficulties because it is hard to know for oneself what is truly beneficial; *moha* or delusion blinds one very often to one's own faults. Of course if a Teacher is not skilled in meditation he may assign an unsuitable subject to a meditator. Some years ago a meditator from Malaysia was seen to have a very long and gloomy face. Upon being asked what was his trouble he replied that he could not put his heart into his university studies which all appeared to be meaningless - 'After all', he said, 'everything is impermanent'. When asked he admitted that he meditated every day on the impermanence of mind-body. The next question to him was 'Do you want to become a novice or a monk?' When he replied in the negative, he was advised to change his meditation subject to loving-kindness. The change in his face over the next week or two was good to see!

Then there was the tense individual, quite good at meditation but rather erratic and with strong tendencies to fear and anxiety. He had been advised to practise loving-kindness every day. After a lapse of time, he appeared again so tense that he could not sit still and was

110.   *And One's Heart well Purifying*

smoking like a factory chimney. It appeared from a conversation with him that he had given up loving-kindness practice some weeks ago and was now only doing insight meditation. This combined with strong coffee, university examinations and his tendency to fear, had brought him to the brink of mental imbalance. He had thrown away the very meditation which was helpful to him! This is the work of delusion.

After this list of troubles, a few of the good results can be briefly emphasized. One very noticeable quality that develops is that the meditator shies away from evil-doing. Meditators find that they become much more sensitive to wrong conduct in themselves and more easily keep to the precepts. Others' wrong actions they become more tolerant of, or they have more equanimity towards them or greater ability to deal with them skilfully, according to what should be done in particular situations. But their own tendencies to break the Precepts become weaker as the 'world-guardians' in them strengthen. These 'world-guardians', who would be assumed by an Indian to be gods, are actually the Buddha's name for *moral shame* and *fear of the results of evil-doing*. The first of them means that one would not like loved and respected people such as Teachers, parents and friends, to know of what one is tempted to do, so one is restrained by that shame and does not do what the defilements urge. Sometimes shame is not strong enough and then the way of restraint is rather the fear of consequences - 'I'm making this kamma but what's the result going to be?' As it will be painful and one does not want to suffer so restraint arises. The usual way of the world though is shamelessness and lack of fear regarding consequences - then the world degenerates as people follow every prompting of the defilements. And how much dukkha follows!

When one is disinclined to break precepts then all good dhammas grow; loving-kindness, compassion, strong effort - and all the rest which a meditator needs. A person like this becomes keen on Dhamma - likes to talk about it and give it more time for practice. Whenever there is a chance to ask questions and learn more such a person does so. It is also characteristic of them to invite correction from Teachers, and to be very helpful, always looking for an opportunity to lend a hand, and asking if they see nothing to do 'What can I help with?' Generosity is something which grows as one gains good results from Dhamma so a person like this never comes empty-handed.

Rapture or *piti* is another factor which increases among meditators. Its different intensities have been mentioned in Chapter Four. Here it can be said that rapture is certainly wholesome but clinging to it or indulging in it is not. Powerful rapture arises at the base of the spine and can travel upwards, a fact indicated by the similes in Chapter Four, and advice upon how this should be channelled is best got from a Teacher. In Hinduism this powerful rapture goes under the name of *Kundalini* and leads to the progressive purification of various centres in the body. This should not be played with! People who do so, having no deep spiritual aim and no good advice from a Teacher often suffer very much from their rash attempts to do things with this rapture. Kundalini-yoga should only be practised if one has competent advice. Even then, it is far better to practise the Buddha's way of steady and natural development through mindfulness rather than forcing the pace. Rapture, if it arises during meditation or at other times, should just be regarded with mindfulness, then attachment to it will not be strengthened. And it should not be made the subject of meditation, as it is itself a meditation-result and not a cause for more development.

Finally, when some serious dukkha strikes at the body or causes a change in one's surroundings, the meditator has some degree of equanimity and patience and can accept the kind of trouble which cannot be righted. Then one can reflect as the Bodhisatta, the Buddha-to-be, did on the death of his wife: 'That which is subject to death has died, that which is subject to destruction is destroyed.'[3]

NOTES TO CHAPTER VI

[1] Middling Discourses (Majjhima-nikāya), No. 4 On Fear and Dread, Ven. Nyanamoli Thera. See *A Treasury of the Buddha's Words* (B.P.S., Kandy).
[2] These four and eight individuals are discussed in the last Chapter.
[3] Jataka 328.

And One's Heart well Purifying

VII

DANGERS TO MEDITATION

The author remembers reading an old western Buddhist book where considerable stress was laid on the fact that 'Meditation is Dangerous"! Well, it is so only if wrongly practised, with the wrong motives or lacking a proper basis in oneself. Those who do not meditate at all are much more dangerous to themselves and others, than meditators are to themselves!

In this Chapter, which is really a continuation of the last one, various dangers will be examined which are not the results of meditation. They are all things which the sincere meditator needs to beware of, or else trouble will surely follow.

First, a danger which cannot be stressed enough is the lack of right motivation for the practice of meditation. When the Eightfold Path is described, the wisdom section comes first headed by Right View and this is followed by Right Motivation (or Intention), thus emphasizing that emotional roots must support clear understanding. These roots, the way in which Right Motivation is always described, are those of renunciation (non-greed), goodwill and non-violence (non-aversion), while of course Right View is the third wholesome root - of wisdom or non-delusion. If one approaches Buddhist meditation with neither Right View regarding dukkha and its cessation, nor with Right Motives of non-greed and non-aversion, then one's meditation is liable to go seriously astray.

Lack of attention to precepts or virtue has been emphasized already but it cannot be mentioned too many times. When the precepts are deliberately broken then the mind is disturbed and meditation will not go smoothly. In particular, intoxicants and drugs should be avoided since they cause mental states to deteriorate. One man who calls himself a Zen Buddhist has defended the use of marihuana on the grounds that it was not mentioned by the Buddha in the Fifth Precept! Perhaps he has never seen a proper explanation of the words of that precept. Sura means distillations, such as brandy, rum, gin, whisky   Meraya covers all fermentations, like beer and wine. Majja includes all the rest whether smoked, sniffed, rubbed on or injected, anything which intoxicates in fact. And one must assume that hemp was well-known in the Buddha's days in India though perhaps not directly mentioned by him. It has been used to stimulate visions of the gods, as it is still used by many Hindu Sadhus (wandering ascetics), for countless centuries. But such methods of obtaining 'highs' have nothing to commend them for Buddhists who would rather place their confidence in steadily developed mindfulness.

Then there are married people who want to meditate because of the amount of conflict they experience but still want to go on playing around with other men and women. The writer even heard of one who had a pact with his wife that his 'allowable' ladies should not be within five miles of his front door! It was strange to observe how upset he became when his wife decided that she too could have a few allowable lovers at a safe distance. Such arrangements however 'liberated' they sound in theory just do not work when it comes to the emotions. Only jealousy and anger can be the result of them - and they will be an end of one's meditation!

Some others have taken up meditation as a way to invest themselves with power so that they could easily sway or hypnotize disciples. 'Power-tripping' certainly does not go with loving-kindness and compassion! Nor with virtue and the development of Right View and wisdom! It leads only to strengthening the defilements, particularly possessiveness and anger, as well as the building up of fear. In fact, it leads to real paranoid states, as can be seen in the relations between many 'gurus' and their disciples.

Power is a most dangerous thing because often it is not guided by virtue. It can be turned either to the bright wholesome side or to darkness, and under the power of the defilements it is likely to be turned to the latter for the purpose of self-glorification, a strengthening of conceit which can go so far that the guru believes himself to be God Almighty or at least a Saviour sent down by him! There are several prominent examples of this among cult-leaders to be seen in our own days. But even one step along this power-tripping path is dangerous for meditators. This is where having a good Teacher for guidance is really helpful.

From power generally we may pass on to powers of the occult variety. The Buddha and some of the Arahants possessed them and a thorough knowledge can be found among great Theravada Teachers down to the present day, as attested by the life of Ven. Acharn Mun (Bhuridatta Mahathera) in Thailand. But they have never been the goal of meditation practice, they are only sidelines which may be experienced by some people. Those who cultivate only the mindfulness forms of practice leading to insight (*vipassanā*) will not have any knowledge of them and even some Arahants, 'dry-visioned' as they are called, have no special abilities. But people who develop calm (*samatha*) often have strange experiences and start to gain various powers. They should not be cultivated! Just be aware with full mindfulness of the unusual occurrence and then return to the normal meditation subject. If such things occur in daily life do not follow them up, gossip about them with others or become fascinated by them! Where they become troublesome, advice is needed from a competent Teacher. he is the only person who should be told of such things.

There is a vast variety of books dealing with the occult and magic these days, and many groups practising such things: all are better left alone! Their motivation is seldom a proper one so that results will be confused. Apart from lack of virtue and emphasis on power, the results of calm - rapture, visions and strange abilities, can easily be taken as complete and final attainment. When a meditator believes that he has reached this then of course there is nothing further that need be done!

In Buddhist tradition the classical example of a monk who went wrong because of magical powers was Devadatta, the Buddha's cousin. He would effect various shape-changing transformations on himself and appear and disappear at will but the only thing he grew in as a result was conceit. So great did this become that he asked the Buddha to step down and allow him to be the Buddha and when Gotama declined this request Devadatta caused a schism in the Sangha and tried acting out the Buddha's role, very unsuccessfully as it turned out. Later, his envy and conceit drove him to try to murder the Buddha three times. By the time he reached this strength of defilements all his powers left him. His end was not inspiring, thought he did have the intention to ask the Buddha for forgiveness. He is always used as a grim warning of where the quest for powers can lead.

Ven. Mahā-Moggallāna, the Luddha's chief left-hand disciple, did possess far greater powers but he was an Arahant and only used them for teaching Dhamma. The Buddha himself, while possessing a full range of 'supernormal success' rarely made use of them, preferring more normal ways of teaching Dhamma. Only when they could not succeed did he use some special method. Buddhist Teachers follow this line down to the present day. The meditator should learn from this that while still trying to practise, and while not yet enlightened, powers are a danger and should not be played with.

Another thing not to be toyed with by a meditator is contacting spirits, or believing that one can do so. Some meditators reach a point where they begin to hear a voice or voices and then come to believe that they have a 'spirit guide'. It may be that some being external to themselves is communicating with them but the chances are just as great that the voice is part of their own minds, a whispering of the subconscious. Now even if a deva wishes to tell one something it will rarely have anything to do with calm and insight practice. Most likely it will just be a distraction away from this. And then the knowledge imparted may be more or less confused according to the mind of the being contacted, for the devas are not enlightened. Of course, if it is just produced by oneself then we again have the situation of blindly believing in the workings of one's own mind. It is better not to be involved in such delusion.

Though occultism has been dealt with already, 'black magic' has not been mentioned in so many words. If 'black' means evil, and gaining power for evil ends or by evil forces, then there is no question what a meditator should do. Keep away! Such things can only be 'dark kamma with a dark result', exactly the way to increase dukkha and grow the defilements, not to speak of other beings' sufferings. And one who practises black magic will be *a person going from brightness to darkness* as far as the next life is concerned.[1]

And though some will protest, this seems the best place to touch on another danger, now well-known as 'tantricism' or 'tantric practice'. These remarks are not intended to apply to those who have devoted themselves to tantric practice within the bounds of a tradition emphasizing virtue and compassion. They may have, to guide them on the Path, a Teacher whose actions of speech and body cannot be blamed. Rather these words are for those who read the many books on the subject which usually emphasize heavily the erotic side and then take to playing 'tantrik' games often with members of the opposite sex. This can never be called a path of purification. However, it has a great appeal because it appears that one *can* have one's cake and eat it too. It *seems* that it is possible to gain great power and wisdom while indulging in erotic pleasures. And it must be said that the original tantric texts themselves are to blame for this misapprehension. They certainly do speak of, for instance, developing the highest bliss while in union with a beautiful girl of sixteen years, or even with one's sister or mother, the principle being that one should use defilements to conquer defilements, in this case, lust to overcome lust. Though Tantric scholars are quick to point out that this is all symbolic and framed in esoteric language called 'twilight speech' so that one should not take the words at their face value, still this is what ordinary people do. The result is an increase in debauchery, something which western society, already bogged down to the axles with sensuality, could certainly do without! It is notable that societies where tantricism has flourished have become enmeshed in a superstitious net of magic, signs and omens and that such an attitude has undoubtedly conduced to their destruction, as happened both with the Indian mediaeval kingdoms and Tibet. Moral conduct and virtue strengthen society while shame and fear of evil-doing, as the Buddha emphasized, are the Guardians of the World.

In contrast to the 'twilight speech' of the tantric texts the words of the Buddha, the Kinsman of the Sun as he was called, are clear and unambiguous. Here are a few words of his from the Pali Canon which show the impossibility of tantric claims: 'Monks, it is impossible indeed that one can pursue (the objects of) sexual gratification without sexual desire, without memories of sexual desire, without thoughts of sexual desire.'[2] And kāma, meaning internal desires, is an unwholesome factor of the mind. Moreover, the Buddha does not at all agree that defilements can be overcome by more defilement - only by the growth of mindfulness and wisdom can they be overcome.

Another danger lies in wealth and commercialism. Dhamma should never be sold. The oral instructions of a Teacher, even written ones in so far as this is practical, should not be made a source of wealth. So practisers of Dhamma who have an ability to teach should not try to get money for their services, while those who are still learning should avoid organisations where some sort of meditative or spiritual teaching is for sale. Any group that advertises and pushes its 'spiritual wares' should be avoided for their interests are guided by greed and not by virtue, meditation and wisdom.

Conceit may be considered next on the list. The meaning of conceit here is not the ordinary one where one says of a person 'He is so conceited'. It includes this certainly but its range is much greater and more subtle. The Buddha speaks of three kinds of conceit which all have their roots in the most basic conceit (or concept) of all; 'I am'. Out of this are born 'I am greater', 'I am equal' and 'I am less'.

Dangers to Meditation

So one may speak of a superiority conceit, and equality conceit and an inferiority conceit. Of these three types, the last one may prevent a person making any effort at all - 'It's all right for him but how could I do that?' The middle one will effectively prevent learning from those who know more and have practised more - 'Well, who does he think he is? I'm as good as he is any day!' The first one is the most dangerous of all for meditators. Having gained some good experience of meditation practice a person comes to think that he or she knows more than other people, a fact that is betrayed by the tone of voice used and the gestures made. And they may come to believe that their experience was Nibbana, that they are Arahants and so have no more defilements, when actually defilements are very obvious to everyone except themselves. The writer remembers the stifling superiority-conceit of a group of lay meditators who believed that they were all Arahants - and so of course, there was nothing left for them to do! A pitiful situation.

Even if there is no belief that Enlightenment has been attained, conceit can still manifest in 'holier-than-thou' attitudes: 'I make an effort, you...', or, 'I meditate every day, you ...'. Only mindfulness will check such over-estimations of oneself.

It is noticeable that when people come out with some particular conceited view or attitude there is an uncomfortable silence because everyone finds conceit that is too blatant hard to handle. It makes for an awkward situation, which translated into Buddhist terms means an increase of dukkha. Conceit is the last fetter shed before Enlightenment but all the way through practice it needs to be watched carefully.

From conceit (=conceptualization) are born views which are basically concepts. The root-conceit 'I am' branches out into a myriad views, many varieties of which were described by the Buddha. Views, which the Buddha called 'the thicket of views, the wilderness of views, the distortion of views, the vacillation of views, the fetter of views', support the concept of self, for which reason many people are very sensitive when their own views are disputed. The concept of self also implies the holding of views so that Teachers in Thailand often speak of a person who is confused in this way as being *mana-diṭṭhi*, a person of conceit-and views, a person hard or impossible to train. If a person is not willing to put down his load of views he cannot see the Dhamma. If his head is burdened with God-concepts, self and soul concepts, exclusivist concepts such as 'Only this is right, everything else is wrong', as the brahmins of the Buddha's day believed, or superiority concepts such as 'Our way is superior, your way is inferior', then, so full of conceit, the Dhamma has no room there! It is interesting to reflect that this superiority-inferiority conceit has actually found its way into Buddhist religion in the guise of the Great Vehicle (Mahāyāna) and the Low Vehicle (Hīnayāna), two words that the Buddha could never have uttered as he was completely free of conceit. An intelligent person can quickly guess who invented such terms.[3] (*Hīna* is a derogatory term and does not mean little or lesser). The tangle of views!

Conceit may be said to be the bane of Buddhists, the most

dangerous among all the defilements. In other religions where there is worship of God or Gods much humility may be developed from the contemplation of being the mere creation of an all-powerful Creator. But Buddhists have no such views and practices, instead all their Path depends on efforts made by themselves, efforts with virtue, efforts with concentration, efforts with insight-wisdom. With the guidance of good Teachers these efforts do not result in an increase of conceit but without such guidance this often happens. This is where Buddhism cannot really be called, as it has been labelled by some people, 'the do-it-yourself religion'.

The Buddha's Teachings found in the Pali Canon are not difficult for an intelligent person to master. Once the concepts are clear if practice is not done using them as a basis then a Buddhist can become 'one who knows it all' but actually knowing nothing since greed, aversion and delusion are quite unaffected by all that knowledge.

Related to this is the conceit that complexity equals profundity. Because of this people study Abhidhamma for years, or they become involved in one of the branches of Buddhist 'philosophy', meaning the scholastic systems developed outside the Pali Sutta (Discourses) and Vinaya (Discipline) and achieve eminence in their knowledge of that system's complications. They may study Nagarjuna's Middle Path, or Asanga's Mind-only or the interpenetrating philosophy of Hwa-Yen - all these are dangers to actual practice which needs no such complexities. The defiled mind guided by craving, conceit and views is very well able to produce philosophies, which like their western counterparts, get one nowhere in the direction of calm and insight. Mara claps his hands and chuckles: 'I can even lead those practical-minded Buddhists by the nose!' The Buddha called philosophizing a variety of 'conceptual proliferation' (papañca) and declared it to be the way of bondage, while the path to Enlightenment consists of the letting go of concepts until the time of Enlightenment comes when one is called nippapañca free of conceptual proliferation, free of views, theories and beliefs.

One view which may be mentioned here as it is fairly well-known in the Buddhist world is that 'Only insight is necessary' to which is sometimes added 'The practice of calm is non-Buddhist'. Both these are extreme statements and do not take account of the differences between personalities. For a few people, such as those who are as brilliant as Ven. Sariputta, the Buddha's right-hand chief disciple, only insight need be cultivated because calm has been developed already. Most people though require the strength of calm before they can stand the scrutiny of insight.

Insight meditation means that one is ready to let go of some or all defilements, and all concepts even. So if one has no deep renunciation spirit the development of insight is not possible, or if it is pushed too rapidly the result will be strong anxiety and much turbulence in the mind.

Desire for 'instant' vipassanā or insight is the result of impetuosity, lack of patience and is related to the presence of strong aversion and weak loving-kindness. The virtue of patience has already been praised in the story of the Patience-preacher, and by the Simile of the Saw (Chapter V.) There is no way that maturity in the Dhamma can be hurried: one just has to keep practising, to practise for calm and insight regularly every day.

Where loving-kindness is not sufficiently developed much fear and anxiety may arise, a danger in that it destroys calm. Loving-kindness is really needed when one lives in secluded meditation retreats whether for a long period or a short one. The snakes and spiders, scorpions and centipedes should all receive one's loving-kindness, otherwise the mind is disturbed by them and no concentration is developed. An example of how not to do it was what happened to a young westerner in a forest Wat in north-east Thailand. He had arrived with high hopes of ordination as a monk and soon after, as a step in this direction he had his head shaved and put on white cloth, undertaking to keep the Eight Precepts. He was given his own wooden hut and divided his time between helping the monks with the Wat's upkeep and his own walking and sitting meditation. One evening having walked up and down for an hour or two, he entered the hut for sitting practice. As there were no flyscreens on the windows he had to sit under his net to escape from the hungry hordes of mosquitoes. When just ready to meditate he saw on the *outside* of his net a very large spider. Thinking 'That must not stay in my hut' he got up and shooed it out with a broom. Then he settled down again to meditate. But this time, on a cupboard some feet away from his net he saw another similar spider. Again he ejected it and then crawled back into the net and having folded his legs, began to meditate. After an hour or so lethargy and drowsiness overcame him and he slid into sleeping position. The quiet night with only soft cicada noises was shattered at about eleven o'clock by the most piercing screams! Everyone rushed to his hut. They called out 'What's the matter?' After a while a sleepy and sheepish head appeared in the doorway saying, 'It was only a dream!' The next day the Teacher ordered him to relate what had happened. He said that after going to sleep he dreamt of an enormous spider twenty or thirty feet high which was out to get him. The Teacher laughed and commented: 'Not enough loving-kindness!'

Indulging in fantasies, an aspect of delusion, is also a danger to meditation. With some people who practise it seems as though it becomes a line of defence for the ego. Sometimes the fantastic situations produced by the confused mind in dreams are clung to and elaborated in the waking state. Sometimes through lack of mindfulness the mind is allowed to drift off into some never-never land of desire. These days there are so many books of fantasy available to take the mind away from what really exists. But the way out of dukkha is not be way of fantasies. It is by seeing things as they really are.

Dreams should not be clung to, nor should one try to interpret them. Mostly they are confused bits of perception tacked together by a rather unmindful and poorly-organized level of mind. Rather develop mindfulness as much as possible in the waking state so that the time one is awake is increased and the time for sleeping decreased. Then dreams will appear less frequently while one's sleep will be deeper and less disturbed.

The last danger to be mentioned is straining at meditation. A lot of people could benefit from making more effort but there are some who try too hard. It seems that they hope to storm the Gates of Heaven! But all that results is various kinds of mental and physical dukkha. Effort, as was emphasized in describing the balance of the faculties (Chapter IV.1.) must be moderate, meaning in accordance with the state of one's spiritual development and with one's opportunities for practice. A suitable practice for those who incline to push meditation too fast is the exercise on the four postures (Chapter III.1.b.), especially the aspect of 'only sitting when sitting'. That is, the meditator should not be trying to meditate, concentrate or strain at anything. Only sit! Just sit and be aware of that! There is nothing to achieve, or to be won. It is not a case of succeeding or failing as though one was taking an examination or test. This practice, 'only sitting while sitting', will not lead to insight directly but as the over-energetic meditator first needs calm it is quite suitable for producing this. After calm has been experienced then the impermanence and so on of that calm can be investigated. This bare awareness of the posture of sitting, a practice which does not try to get anything is similar to the Soto Zen way of just sitting (*shikantaza*). This kind of meditator needs a little of Taoist 'non-doing' otherwise his meditation cannot succeed. But Taoist non-doing is not for everyone and it can be heard recommended by people who certainly need to make a great deal of effort. Another one of those traps!

To conclude this chapter and change metaphor as well, the Buddha spoke of ten thorns which can pierce meditators and destroy their practice:

> There are these ten thorns. What ten? Love of company is a thorn to a lover of seclusion. Devotion to the sign of beauty is a thorn to one devoted to contemplating the sign of unattractiveness in the body. Seeing shows is a thorn to one guarding his sense-doors. The vicinity of women is a thorn to one leading the Holy Life.[4] Noise is a thorn to the first jhana. Initial application and sustained application is a thorn to the second jhana. Rapture is a thorn to the third jhana. In-breaths and out-breaths are a thorn to the fourth jhana. Perception and feeling are a thorn to the attainment of the cessation of perception and feeling. Lust is a thorn, aversion is a thorn, delusion is a thorn. Dwell without thorns, monks, dwell thornless! The Arahants are without thorns, monks, the Arahants are thornless![5]

NOTES TO CHAPTER VII

1. The Buddha spoke of four types of persons: going from dark to bright, dark to dark, bright to dark, bright to bright. A meditator should be in the last class.
2. See *The Snake Simile* trans. Nyanaponika Thera, Wheel 48/49, B.P.S., Kandy.
3. Western Buddhists who are caught up in the tangle of conceit-and-views around Mahayana-Hinayana should laugh themselves out of it by considering how it would be if they had the chance to approach a Buddha, perhaps the last one, Gotama, saying, 'Excuse me, Sir, but are you a Great Vehicle Buddha or a Low Vehicle Buddha?' He might reply with a simile: '"Divine Vehicle" is the name for the Noble Eightfold Path; and so is "Dhamma-Vehicle"; and so is "Peerless Victory in Battle"; for all the components of the Noble Eightfold Path culminate in the expulsion of lust, aversion and delusion.' Samyutta-nikaya XLV. 4 trans. Ven. Nyanamoli.
4. The vicinity of men would be a thorn to a woman leading the celibate life but there the Buddha was addressing monks.
5. Adapted from *The Life of the Buddha*, p. 168, (B.P.S., Kandy).

This is the Buddha's Teaching

VIII

THE FRUITS OF PENETRATION

In this concluding chapter the fruits of penetration are mostly conveyed in quotations from the words of the Buddha and some of his enlightened disciples, with a few notes added by the author. It is as though these fruits are reflected here in the mirror of the Buddha's words - with a sprinkling of dust which is all that can be added here. Those who want to know what those fruits look like more directly are advised to read a modern account of an Enlightened monk's life by which they may be inspired to reach out a hand to grasp them[1]. But there are a few others who will not be content until they taste them. Paradoxically they will find that these fruits cannot be grasped and the savour of them comes only to the tongue of one who no longer desires them. Indeed, there is no fruit to taste and no taster to desire. These people had better go for longer or shorter periods as their lives permit, to stay with living Enlightened Masters.[2] Then they may taste the incomparable flavour of the Dhamma's fruits.

The first quotation, from the Dhammapada, emphasizes that the Further Shore of Nibbana, or Arahantship, is not known by many people in this present life. Though all the factors necessary for it - the three characteristics which are ever present in mind and body - are at hand, yet the effort to be made is a great one. This is conveyed in these verses when they speak of going forth from home to homelessness as a monk or nun, something which cannot be done by many people even though it is most conducive for Dhamma-practice.

> Among men they are few
> who go to the Further Shore,
> most among mankind
> run about this hither shore.
> But they indeed who practise Dhamma
> according to Dhamma well-expounded,
> they among men will go across
> Death's Realm so hard to pass.
> Abandoning the dhammas dark
> the wise should cultivate the bright;
> having from home to homeless gone
> hard to enjoy is solitude -
> Let him desire that rare delight,
> renouncing pleasure, owning naught;
> that wise man should cleanse himself
> from defilements of the mind.
> Who in true Bodhi's qualities
> the mind well-grown, perfected,
> who delights, no longer clinging,

The Fruits of Penetration

in relinquishing attachment,
they free of taints and radiant
in this world attain Nibbana.   (1)

Bodhi is Enlightenment, the complete awakening of a Buddha or an Arahant, but there are three degrees before this when glimpses of Nibbana are obtained. All those who have had such glimpses so that their defilements have lessened and the troublesome self-views fallen away, are called Noble Ones. They are all mentioned in the following passage as 'great beings' who inhabit the ocean of the Buddha Dhamma and discipline.

> Again, just as the Great Ocean is the abode of great beings - there are such beings in it as whales, sea-serpents, demons, monsters, and tritons,...so too this Dhamma and Discipline is the abode of great beings - there are such beings in it as the Stream-winner and he who has entered on the way to the fruit of Stream-winning, the Once-returner, and he who has entered on the way to the fruit of Once-returning; the Non-returner, and he who has entered on the way to the fruit of Non-returning; the Arahant, and he who has entered on the way to the fruit of Arahantship.   (2)

This passage seems to make distinctions between a Stream-winner and one who has only the Path or Way to that attainment. Such a seeming distinction is made in the frequently recited passage recollecting the virtues of the Noble Sangha - all those monks, nuns, and lay-men and women disciples, who have in-seen the Dhamma-truth, where it says 'The four pairs of men, the eight types of persons'. But for practical purposes only four types of Noble Ones are counted. Though in the next quotation they are mentioned as monks (because at that time the Buddha was referring to the Sangha of monks), they may be nuns or lay-people of either sex.

> There are monks who with the exhaustion of the first three fetters have entered the stream, are no more subject to perdition, certain of rightness, and destined to enlightenment. There are monks who, with the exhaustion of three fetters and the attenuation of lust, hate and delusion are Once-returners; returning once to this world they will make an end of dukkha. There are monks who, with the destruction of the five more immediate fetters are destined to reappear spontaneously elsewhere and will there, finally attain Nibbana, never returning meanwhile from that world. There are monks who are Arahants with taints exhausted, who have lived out the life, done what was to be done, laid down the burden, reached the highest goal, destroyed the fetters of being, and who are completely liberated through final knowledge.   (3)

'Entering the stream' - going to Enlightenment, is the name for the first experience of penetrating Dhamma, sometimes because of the intensity and depth of meditation practice but sometimes because the mind becomes fully attentive when listening to Dhamma. The three fetters abandoned are: the view of aggregates as self, sceptical doubt, and adherence to mere rites and vows. The first of these does not imply a full penetration of not-self but just removes one leg, views, of the tripod - craving, conceit, views - on which the self-concept (conceit) rests. Sceptical doubt the second fetter, which prevents practice and attainment, vanishes as Nibbana is glimpsed in the Path-moment. After this a Stream-winner can never take any other Teacher than the Buddha, nor follow any other practice apart from his Dhamma, and never give his heart to any body of religious apart from the Sangha. The third fetter is adherence to mere rites and vows, that is, the Stream-winner does not cling to such things as matters central to religion. When people adhere fanatically to ritual or to the performance of certain vows as essential for salvation even persecution and murder have been the results. The Stream-winner by seeing that the essence of religion is not self drops all concern with such matters. It does not mean, of course, that such a person no longer pays respect in the usual way, or no longer recites the homage to the Triple Gem - Buddha, Dhamma, Sangha; actually his faith in these becomes unshakeable because he has had a wisdom-experience to back it up. And his moral conduct is unblameable since he does not stray from the Five Precepts. Another advantage is that he is 'no more subject to perdition' he cannot be reborn in any subhuman state; 'certain of rightness' - he must gain human or super-human (deva) birth; 'destined to enlightenment' - he is sure to win Arahantship in seven lives at most.

Here is an account of a layman attaining stream-entry:

> Then the Blessed One gave the householder Upāli progressive instruction, that is to say, talk on giving, on virtue, on the heavens; he explained the danger, the degradation and the defilement in sensual desires, and the blessings in renunciation. When he knew that the householder Upāli's mind was ready, receptive, free from hindrance, elated and confident, he expounded to him the teaching peculiar to the Enlightened Ones: Dukkha, its origin, its cessation and the path. Just as a clean cloth with all marks removed would take dye evenly, so too, while the householder Upāli sat there, the spotless immaculate vision of the Dhamma arose in him: 'All that is subject to arising, is subject to cessation'. Then the householder Upāli saw and reached and knew and fathomed the Dhamma; he crossed beyond doubt, he had done with questioning, gained intrepidity and became independent of others in the Teacher's Dispensation... (4)

The tradition of wholehearted attention to the deep Dhamma spoken by meditation masters is still alive in South-east Asia now and in the quiet of the night while they expound the way of enlightenment, given under the five headings of progressive instruction above, no doubt some still see the Dhamma in their hearts.

The Fruits of Penetration 125.

A famous Teacher in Bangkok, the late Venerable Phra Upaligunupamacariya (Chan Chandupamo) said, 'If a Buddhist fails to win the Fruit of Stream-entry in this life he has wasted his entire existence'. The Buddha praised this attainment above the possession of all worldly things:

> Than o'er the earth sole sovreignty,
> than going unto heaven,
> than lordship over all the worlds:
> better the Stream-winner's Fruit. (5)

The Once-returner has only one more birth as a human being during which he will reach Arahantship. Only one more birth is possible for such a person because not only have the three fetters dropped off but greed and aversion have been greatly weakened. Both Stream-winners and Once-returners may be lay people leading the usual sort of family life. They do not make their attainments conspicuous by telling people; boastfulness is a sure indication of non-attainment. The only thing such people have attained to is increased delusion! But one might notice a great deal of unfanatical, quiet devotion, steady practice and good moral conduct. Increased too with the lessening of self-centredness is loving-kindness and compassion, while the Once-returner would seldom show greed or aversion and be possessed of much equanimity.

All the five lower fetters listed in the next passage are abandoned completely by the Non-returner, who is contrasted with our normal state:

> An untaught ordinary man who disregards Noble Ones...lives with his heart possessed and enslaved by the embodiment view, by sceptical doubt, by adherence to rites and vows, by lust for sensuality and by ill-will, and he does not see how to escape from them when they arise: these, when they are habitual and remain uneradicated in him, are called the more immediate fetters. (6)

When these five fetters have all gone as there is no 'lust for sensuality' any more, the celibate holy life becomes natural for such a person. If married then a Non-returner gives choice to the marriage partner to stay and share the holy life or go and find happiness with some man or woman. A Non-returner may continue in lay life but obviously it will be one which is marked by non-possessiveness and great loving-kindness as there is no way that anger can arise again.

And there is no way in which such a one can be reborn again among human beings. They must experience a final birth among the devas of the Pure Abodes and there attain Nibbana. When all sensuality has been abandoned there is nothing to return here for. The Pure Abodes are subtle and refined levels of the Brahma-world which correspond to the subtle and fine mental-emotional state of the Non-returner at the time of death.

The Buddha commenting on the attainment of Non-returning by a monk, praised it in this verse:

> One with a wish for the Undeclared,
> with a mind exhilarated,
> a mind unbound from pleasures of sense,
> an 'Upstream-goer' he is called. (7)

'The Undeclared' is Nibbana which is fully known by the Arahant. Whereas the other three types of Noble Ones have only a glimpse of Nibbana each time a Path-moment is experienced, the Arahant as he has abandoned all the fetters, the five further ones given below as well, can enjoy Nibbana whenever he wishes.

The five more remote fetters are: attachment to (subtle) form, attachment to formlessness, conceit ('I am'), distraction and ignorance. (8)

With the abandoning of the first two rebirth in the realms of subtle form and formlessness become impossible. There is nowhere to be reborn and there is no one to be reborn either as the conceit 'I am' has been relinquished. Even the slight restlessness produced by subtle forms of ego-clinging now disappears. Ignorance, which always means in the Buddha's teachings, 'ignorance of the Noble Truths', has no place in the Arahant's mind as those Truths have been thoroughly penetrated by him. In this way he has 'destroyed the fetters of being' (becoming) and there is nothing further for him to do. The burden, which was discussed in Chapter VI.4, has been laid down and another is not taken up.

This great grasped-at burden when finally laid down ensures a life of wisdom and compassion without any clinging. Such a life would indeed be hard for one still living the household life, therefore the homeless life of a monk or nun fits the attainment of Arahantship much better. This becomes clearer when we consider the nine things that it is impossible for an Arahant to do:

He cannot purposely kill a living being, nor take by way of theft what is not given, nor indulge in sexual intercourse, nor speak falsehood in full awareness, nor make a store of things for his own enjoyment, as he did formerly when a householder, while the last four factors are that he cannot go astray through bias towards desire, aversion, delusion or fear.[4]

In other words, though passed beyond making any kind of kamma yet his actions would always seem to the unenlightened to be wholesome: he never exhibits the unwholesome as he has not the slightest tendency towards it left, all the unwholesome roots have vanished. It is possible for this kind of person to live in the community of the monks' or nuns' Sangha but it would be almost impossible to lead a householder's life.

If we examine the transition from Non-returner to Arahant in the light of another passage, we can see how subtle is the conceit 'I am' and how difficult it is to be rid of it.

The Fruits of Penetration

(Questioned by senior monks, the Venerable Khemaka said): I do not see in these five clung-to aggregates any self or anything belonging to self...Yet I am not an Aharant with the taints exhausted. On the contrary, I still have the attitude 'I am' with respect to these clung-to aggregates, though I do not see 'I am this' with respect to them...I do not say 'I am form' or 'I am feelings' or 'I am perception' or 'I am apart from consciousness'; yet I still have the attitude 'I am' with respect to the five clung-to aggregates although I do not see 'I am this' with respect to them. Although a Noble Disciple may have abandoned the five more immediate fetters, still his conceit 'I am', desire 'I am', underlying-tendency 'I am', with respect to the five clung-to aggregates remains as yet unabolished. Later he abides contemplating rise and fall thus: 'Such is form, such its origin, such its disappearance' (and the same with the other four aggregates), till by doing so, his conceit 'I am' eventually comes to be abolished.' (9)

The last sentence gives the method for abandoning the last traces of 'I am', that is, the contemplation of the five aggregates as they arise and pass away (see Chapter III.4) until they are all seen as void of self, a theme we shall return to later.

Here is the Buddha again speaking on conceit of self and the one who has passed beyond it, the Silent Sage or Arahant. He is called 'silent' because he has no ideas of self-reference within, not because he keeps silent and does not speak, an ascetic practice condemned by the Buddha.

'I am' is a conceit, 'I am this' is a conceit, 'I shall be' is a conceit, 'I shall not be' is a conceit, 'I shall be possessed of form' is a conceit, 'I shall be formless' is a conceit, 'I shall be percipient', is a conceit, 'I shall be non-percipient' is a conceit, 'I shall be neither-percipient-nor-non-percipient' is a conceit.[5] Conceit is a disease, conceit is a cancer, conceit is a dart. It is with the surmounting of all conceits that one is called a Silent Sage. The Sage who is Silent neither is reborn, nor ages, nor dies, he is unassailed and free from longing. He has none of that whereby he might be reborn. Not being reborn, how shall he age? Not ageing, how shall he die? Not dying, how shall he be assailed? Being unassailed, what shall he long for? So it was with reference to this that it was said 'Steadied whereon no more the tides of conceit occur in him, and when the tides of conceit occur in him no more, he is called a Silent Sage.' (10).

A verse from the Sutth-nipāta and a prose Sutta passage convey much the same picture of one who is at peace, not just with the world, not just with himself, but at peace because there is no self:-

And he who has considered all the contrasts on this earth, and is no more disturbed by anything whatever in the world, the Peaceful One, freed from rage, from sorrow, and from longing, he has passed beyond birth and decay.   (11)

And for a disciple thus freed, in whose heart dwells peace, there is nothing to be added to what has been done, and naught more remains for him to do.[6] Just as a rock of one solid mass remains unshaken by the wind, even so neither forms, nor sounds, nor smells, nor tastes, nor touches, of any kind, neither the desired nor the undesired, can cause such a one to waver. Steadfast is his mind, gained is deliverance..   (12)

So far we have reviewed the Arahant's attainments in the light of the ten fetters and conceit particularly. Now we may get another glimpse of him by approaching him through the Sutta-teaching of the three taints which emphasizes the importance of the foundations of mindfulness.

There are these three taints, the taint of sensuality, the taint of desire for renewed existence, and the taint of ignorance. For getting rid of these three taints, the four foundations of mindfulness should be cultivated.   (13)

The taints, (poisons, pollutions are other translations for $\bar{a}sava$) are the deepest layer of distortion in the mind, the last and strongest barrier of the defilements. When defilements lead people to break the Precepts they are then most obvious and coarsest. A refined level of defilements is seen in the Five Hindrances which have already been discussed (Chapter IV.2) but the most subtle of all are the taints.

The taint of sensuality is hardly recognised by most people as 'tainted' - it is just normal for the mind to be stimulated by sensory impressions. The more of them there are the more the mind is activated and stirred up. But there is a limit to the enjoyment of sensory stimulation and too much is known to produce dukkha. 'Sensuality' in the Pali is *kāma*, a word which covers both the exterior sense stimuli and the desires for this within the heart. Ordinary people live with both and are not aware that there is anything unwholesome. People who take up the training in Dhamma know that sense-restraint is necessary if one is to enjoy a calm mind during meditation and daily life. They restrict the range of sense impressions so that the defilement of sensuality is not activated in the heart. Arahants have no kāma left in their hearts though of course they perceive the world through the senses. The exterior kāma has no interior kāma to adhere to. They can therefore appreciate the beauties of nature, evident from many of their verses, without any stimulation of desire and greed.

When this taint has gone rebirth would no longer be possible in the kāma-world - the realm of sensuality in which human beings and animals live. But with this first taint, *the taint for being*, or the taint of desire for renewed existence, is extinguished as well. Being, or becoming, means 'I am' and 'self', with views and conceit, in some way or other. The Arahant does not want to be, but he does not

The Fruits of Penetration

either want not to be. Ordinary people when they are tired of being, because of too much dukkha, switch over to non-being. From holding eternalistic views of self-soul they swing to the opposite extreme of clinging to views of annihilation after death, or from enjoying life (which conceals the taint for being) they swing over to wishing for death or suicide. The Arahant has no such wavering between extremes: while body and mind continue he lives without grasping; untainted by desires to be or not to be.

The taint of *ignorance* is just another way of speaking of the fetter of ignorance which has been dealt with already. One has always to remember it as *ignorance of the Noble Truths.*

Here is a picture of two Arahants, free of all fetters and taints, praising the four foundations of mindfulness:-

> Once the venerable Anuruddha and the venerable Sariputta lived near Vesali in Ambapali's Grove. In the evening after the venerable Sariputta had emerged from the (day-time) seclusion, he went to the venerable Anuruddha. After he had exchanged with him friendly and polite greetings, he said this to him: 'Your features are radiant, friend Anuruddha, your face is bright and has a pure complexion. What is the mind's abode in which the venerable Anuruddha often dwells?' 'Friend, I often dwell now with my mind firmly established in the four foundations of mindfulness. A monk who is an Arahant, taint-free, who has lived out the Holy Life, done what was to be done, laid down the burden, attained to the goal, destroyed the fetters of existence, and is liberated in perfect wisdom - he frequently dwells with a mind firmly established in the four foundations of mindfulness.' 'It is a gain for us, friend, a great gain, that we have heard that weighty word from the mouth of venerable Anuruddha.' (14)

Even Arahants 'for whom there is nothing to be added to what has been done, and naught remains for him to do' (text 12) still employ the four foundations as a way of 'peaceful abiding here and now'. They find delight in the ocean of Dhamma.

In the next two texts the exhaustion of the three roots of unwholesomeness is called in one, Arahantship, and in the next Nibbana, thus passing from the description of persons to the more abstract principle.

> That which is the exhaustion of lust, of hate and of delusion is called Arahantship. (15)

> At one time venerable Sariputta was living at the village of Nālaka. Then a wanderer called Jambukhādaka approached him and having done so he exchanged polite and courteous greetings with venerable Sariputta, after which he sat down there. When he was seated he said this, 'Friend Sariputta, it is said, Nibbana! Nibbana! Now what is Nibbana?'
> 'Friend, that which is the exhaustion of lust, aversion and delusion is called Nibbana.'

Is there, friend, a path, is there a way of practice for the realization of Nibbana?'
'There is, friend.'
'What is that path or way of practice?'
'This Noble Eightfold Path is for the realization of Nibbana, that is to say: Right View, Right Intention, Right Speech, Right Action, Right Livelihood, Right Effort, Right Mindfulness, Right Concentration.'
'It is a good path, friend, a good way of practice for the realization of Nibbana but it certainly needs diligence.' (16)

Diligence is needed by those who have not yet reached the experience of Nibbana. They are the 'ordinary people' (*puthujjana*) like ourselves. If they believe in the way pictured at the beginning of the passage below then they are called 'foolish ordinary people'. When they cease to aim at their own ruin and that of others by practising Dhamma then they can be labelled 'good ordinary people'. Finally, they come to experience Nibbana in one of the Path-moments when they enter the family of the Noble Ones (Ariya).

Enraptured with lust, enraged with anger, blinded by delusion, overwhelmed, with a mind ensnared, man aims at his own ruin, at the ruin of others, at the ruin of both, and he experiences mental pain and grief. But if lust, anger and delusion are given up, man aims neither at his own ruin, nor at the ruin of others, nor at the ruin of both, and he experiences no mental pain and grief. This is Nibbana, to be seen here and now, not delayed in time, inviting one to come and see, leading inwards and to be known by the wise each for himself. (17)

For the wise and diligent person Nibbana is not a faraway goal but as the Buddha says above 'to be seen here and now' while in the verses below he stresses how it is for all who are in danger of being swept away by the mighty floods of the taints - of sensuality, existence, ignorance and views.

Standing in the middle of the waters
having then great fear of mighty floods
afflicted thus with ageing and with dying
for such as them do I proclaim the Isle.
No attachment and no grasping either,
that is indeed the Isle of No-beyond,
Nibbana, that is what I call it,
the ending both of ageing and of dying. (18)

Here are two famous negative descriptions which show Nibbana as beyond all words to describe. Words are useful for buying and selling, difficult for philosophy, hardly fit meditation states and have no positive way of describing Nibbana.

Monks, there is that sphere where is neither earth nor water,

The Fruits of Penetration

neither fire nor air, nor the sphere of infinite space or that of infinite consciousness, or that of no-thingness, or the sphere of neither-perception-nor-non-perception; not this world, not another world, neither the moon nor the sun. That I say is indeed neither coming nor going nor staying, not passing away and not arising. Unsupported, unmoving, devoid of object - that indeed is the end of dukkha. (19)

Peace it is and Excellence it is, that is to say - the stilling of all conditions, the rejection of all assets (for rebirth),[7] the destruction of craving, passionlessness, cessation, Nibbana. (20)

Turning now from the words that the Buddha used to 'describe' Nibbana, we may understand a little more by considering what he has to say on voidness.

First there is a well-known verse from the Dhammapada:

All the dhammas, not one's self;
when with wisdom one sees this,
then one tires of dukkha -
this is the path to purity. (21)

In Chapter III.(4), the meaning and contemplation of dhammas has been discussed. All of the conditioned dhammas are impermanent in the most subtle sense and therefore unsatisfactory (dukkha). While grasped at as 'I' and 'mine' they will be the source of more dukkha. In this verse the Buddha has pointed out that all grasping at a self is linked to dukkha, whether it is the grasping of the ordinary person at 'his own' mind and body, that of the religious believer at a soul or Higher Self (etc.), the meditator who grasps at a jhana-experience as his purified self, soul, or as God, the Buddhist who analyses the self-concept away but takes no practical measures to in-see the five aggregates with *vipassana* (insight) and so grasps at the theory of Dhamma, or another Buddhist who has analysed events down to dhammas but then gets stuck with a theory of their essences which obstructs the seeing of their emptiness.[8] Not grasping anywhere at all is difficult, yet that is the only way to experience Nibbana which is the Unconditioned Dhamma.

The Buddha makes it clear in the next quotation how voidness and not self are related:

'Void is the world, void is the world!' is said, Lord. In respect of what is it said, 'Void is the world'?

Because it is void of self and what belongs to self therefore the world is called void. And what is void of self and what belongs to self? The eye, ear, nose, tongue, body, mind are void of self and what belongs to self. So are forms, sounds, smells, tastes, touches and thoughts. So are eye-consciousness...(round to) mind-consciousness. So are eye-contact...(round to) mind-contact. So too are the pleasant, painful and neutral feelings that arise dependent on eye-contact...mind-contact, all these are void of self and what belongs to self. (22)

All the dhammas mentioned here are regarded by ordinary people as self and as marked by permanence and solidity. Yet all are revealed by insight meditation to be void of these qualities and in that revelation all grasping comes to an end. The Buddha mentions 'the world' in terms of the six senses round to the types of feeling arising dependent on them. Not only this world but every other state of existence, subhuman, human and superhuman - all are void, as another questioner came to know:-

Mogharāja: About this world, the other world,
the Brahma-world and devas too -
I do not know your view at all
O Gotama of great renown.
This question I have come with
to the One who Sees Beyond:
How should the world be looked at
that the Death-king sees one not?

The Buddha: Ever mindful, see the world
as void, O Mogharaja, Thus
uprooting view of self be one
who crosses over death.
Look at the world in this way
that the Death-king sees one not. (23)

The Death-king, another name for the defilements, cannot persuade a person like this to seek for more birth and death when they have found the Deathless, Nibbana. It is called the Deathless because it is beyond birth and death.[9]

Here is the Buddha again speaking of voidness by using similes for the five aggregates. It should be noted that the third one is usually translated 'perception' and the fourth 'mental formations' while a plantain tree is just a banana 'palm'.

The Kinsmen of the Sun made clear:
form compared to a fleck of foam,
feeling to a bubble compared,
and memory to a mirage,
thought compared to a plantain-tree,
and consciousness to a magical trick. (24)

Flecks of foam floating on a river are not thought of as self or belonging to self, but form (body) is thought of like this even though the elements composing it are similar to those found in foam. Water, inside or outside the body, knows no owner. The same is true of the other great elements, of earth (solidity), fire (temperature) and air (movement).

Feelings too are as empty of self as a bubble, arising and passing as quickly as it does. Perception involving the recognition process,

The Fruits of Penetration 133.

and so, memory, is likened to a mirage, an image that is not really the way that it appears. Mental formations, roughly 'thoughts' have no core or essence of self to them, just as the banana plant lacks even softwood, not to speak of heartwood. Thoughts are like the sheathing of leaves of the banana, one coiled in another but there is no on who is the thinker of them. Last is consciousness which knows the bare impressions - the eye-consciousness knows colour and shape, ear-consciousness knows sound, nose-consciousness knows smell, tongue-consciousness knows taste, body-consciousness knows touch while mind-consciousness knows all the bare impressions of the other five and puts them all together, a magician indeed who conjures up the world. The conjuring of course may be done very well in which case what is perceived will be close to the way things are but when the conjuring tricks are confused by the presence of much defilement then the world known will be far from the truth and beset with much dukkha.

The last part of this chapter concerns the state of one who is Enlightened, a Buddha or an Arahant, after the scattering of the five aggregates at the time of death. In the first passage the Buddha is questioning venerable Anurādha about how he *conceives* of the Tathāgata (one Enlightened). 'Conceiving' is having concepts of, or having conceits about, and involves conceit, as we have described already. The root-conceit (concept) is 'I am', and these questions all concern existence.

> How do you conceive this, Anurādha, do you see form, feeling, perception, mental formations, consciousness, (individually) as the Tathāgata?' 'No, Lord.'
> 'How do you conceive this, do you see that Tathāgata as in form, as apart from form, as in feeling, as apart from feeling, as in perception, as apart from perception, as in mental formations, as apart from mental formations, as in consciousness, as apart from consciousness?' 'No, Lord.'
> 'How do you conceive this, do you see the Tathāgata as form-feeling-perception-mental-formations-consciousness (together)?' 'No, Lord.'
> 'How do you conceive this, do you see the Tathāgata as having no form, feeling, perception, mental formations, consciousness?' 'No, Lord.'
> 'Anurādha, when a Tathāgata is here and now unapprehendable for you as true and established, is it fitting to say of him: "Friends, one who is a Tathāgata, highest of men, supremest of men, attained to the supreme attainment, when a Tathāgata is describing him, he describes him apart from the following four instances: After death a Tathāgata exists (is), or after death a Tathāgata does not exist (is not) or after death a Tathāgata both does and does not exist or after death a Tathāgata neither exists nor does not exist"?' 'No, Lord.' 'Good, good, Anurādha! What I describe, now as formerly, is dukkha and the cessation of dukkha.' (25)

That which is enlightened is not of any of the five aggregates individually, nor them all together, not in them or apart from them. Finally it should not be conceived that the Tathāgata (one attained to Truth) has no form and so on.[10] All these are views which necessarily fall short of the Truth of Dhamma. Even though venerable Anurādha recognizes that the views
 after death an enlightened one exists (is),
 after death an enlightened one does not exist,
 after death an enlightened one both exists and does not exist,
 after death an enlightened one neither exists nor does not exist,
are inadequate he has tried to say to those who questioned him that there is some other way of describing the Buddha or Arahant who has died. The Buddha brings him down to earth with the essence of the Dhamma: the existence of dukkha and the way to its cessation.

In the next quotation the Buddha is conversing with a wanderer called Vacchagotta who is trying to understand what the Buddha teaches in respect of the death of one who is enlightened. Here is an extract of their conversation with the wonderfully profound and stirring Simile of the Fire:

'This Dhamma is profound, hard to see and hard to discover. It is the most peaceful and superior goal of all, unattainable by mere ratiocination, subtle and for the wise to experience. It is hard for you to know it when you belong to another view, another choice, another preference, whose training is different, whose teacher's doctrine is different. So I shall question you here in return, Vaccha. Answer as you choose. What do you think, Vaccha, suppose a fire was burning before you, would you know "This fire is burning before me"?' 'I should, venerable Sir.' 'If someone asked you, Vaccha, "What does this fire burning before you burn dependent on?" what would you answer?' 'I should answer in this way, Master Gotama. "This fire burning before me burns dependent on grass and sticks"'. 'If that fire before you was extinguished, would you know "This fire before me is extinguished?"' 'I should, venerable sir.' 'If someone asked you "In which direction has that fire which is extinguished gone in: the east, west, north or south?" what would you answer?' 'That does not apply, Master Gotama. The fire burnt owing to the grass and sticks (it had to cling to) as fuel; when they are finished up and it has no nutriment because it is not nourished with any more, it is reckoned as "extinguished".' 'So too, Vaccha, when describing a Tathāgata (here meaning anyone fully enlightened such as an Arahant) the form, feeling, perception, mental formations, consciousness, by which he could be described, have been abandoned by a Tathāgata, cut off at the root, made like a palm stump, done away with, so that they are no more liable to future arising. A Tathāgata is liberated from reckonings in terms of form, feeling, perception, mental formations, consciousness, he is profound, immeasurable, as hard to fathom as the ocean: the term "re-arises" does not apply, the term "does not arise" does not apply, the term "both arises and does not arise" does not apply, the term "neither arises nor does not arise" does not apply.' (26)

This does not leave very much to say, and in fact the book's end is very near. 'Arises' (is, exists) is easily understood for it is our state of being-becoming now and involves eternalistic views based on the unwholesome root of greed. 'Does not arise' (is not, does not exist) is also easily understood as the opposite of the first and is based on a nihilistic outlook rooted in aversion. 'Both arises and does not arise' (both is (exists) and is not) is a combination of the first two and would apply for instance to a being whose existence is mental but not physical as the devas of the first three formless realms. The last is the exclusion of the first two and the opposite of the third and seems to point out some subtle alternative such as the devas of the fourth formless realm - neither-perception-nor-non-perception - this also does not apply to an enlightened one after death. Their state was compared to the flame that is extinguished using the same verb which is employed for the extinguishing of the self and the defilements by which it is nourished. Yet their state, for want of a better expression, is not non-existence or annihilation which has already been pointed out as wrong view.

At the time of the Buddha's Final Nibbana (which ordinary people would call death), it was said by one of his close disciples, another Arahant:-

> As the flame itself goes out
> so was the freedom of his heart. (27)

And this same simile was used to a young brahmin who asked the Buddha some questions. Here is the end of their conversation - and the end of this chapter and book as well.

(The Buddha): Just as a flame blown out then disappears,
one cannot calculate what is its state:
the Sage too disappears from body, mind,
one cannot calculate what is his state.

(Upasiva): Does he not exist who's reached the goal?
or does he dwell forever free from ill?
O Sage, do well declare this unto me
For certainly this dhamma's known to you.

(The Buddha): Of him who's reached the goal no measure's found,
there is not that by which he could be named,
when dhammas all for him have been destroyed,
destroyed are all the ways of telling too. (28).

THIS is the Buddha's Teaching.

Sources for Quotations in Chapter VIII.

(1) *The Path of Truth* (Dhammapada), verse 85-89 trans. Khantipalo, Mahamakut Press, Bangkok.
(2) *The Life of the Buddha*, trans. Nyanamoli Thera, A. Eights 20, Buddhist Publication Society, Kandy.
(3) *Middling Discourses*, M. 118, trans. Nyanamoli Thera (MSS).
(4) ibid, 56.
(5) *The Path of Truth*, verse 178.
(6) *Middling Discourses*, M. 64.
(7) *The Path of Truth*, verse 218.
(8) *The Life of the Buddha*, D. 33.
(9) ibid., S. XXII. 89
(10) *Middling Discourses*, M. 140.
(11) *The Word of the Buddha*, Sn. V. 4 Trans. Nyanatiloka Mahathera, B.P.S. Kandy.
(12) ibid., A. Sixes 55.
(13) S. XLVII. 50.
(14) S. LII. 9.
(15) *The Life of the Buddha*, S. XXXVIII. 2
(16) S. XXXVII. 1.
(17) *The Word of the Buddha*, A. Threes 55.
(18) Sn. V. 11.
(19) Ud. VIII. 1.
(20) A. Threes 32.
(21) *The Path of Truth*, verse 279.
(22) *The Life of the Buddha*, S. XXXV. 85.
(23) Sn. V. 16
(24) S. XXII. 95
(25) *The Life of the Buddha*, S. XLIV. 2.
(26) *Middling Discourses*, M. 72.
(27) D. 16.
(28) Sn. v. 7.

In the above list of sources:-

D = Dīgha-nikāya (Long Discourses)
M = Majjhima-nikāya (Middling Discourses)
S = Samyutta-nikāya (Related Discourses
A = Anguttara-nikāya (Numerical Discourses)
Sn = Sutta-nipāta (The Discourse Collection)
Ud = Udāna (Inspired Words).

The Dhammapada verses and the discourses where only a reference number appears have been translated by the author, who is also most grateful for permission freely given by Venerable Nyanaponika Mahathera to quote from the works published by the B.P.S., Kandy, Sri Lanka. Translations by Venerable Nyanamoli Thera in *The Life of the Buddha* and in his MS. of 'Middling Discourses' have been slightly changed for clarifying their meaning.

NOTES TO CHAPTER VIII

1. Among all accounts available in Theravada Buddhist tradition *The Life of Phra Acharn Mun, Meditation Master* is the most inspiring.
2. The tradition which the author is best acquainted with is that of the forest-dwelling monks who are disciples of Phra Acharn Mun in north-east Thailand. An account of the life of such forest monks (and nuns) appears in my *Banner of the Arahants*, B.P.S., Kandy.
3. The Buddha did not of course, call his teaching 'Buddhism', but referred to it as the Dhamma-Vinaya, the Truthful-Law-Teaching-Path (Dhamma), with the Discipline leading one out of dukkha (Vinaya).
4. See Numerical Discourses, Nines, 7.
5. All the future tense conceits refer to conceptualizing about one's state after death.
6. Long after the Buddha's days 'Mahayana' authors formulated ideas that the Arahant still had to tread the Bodhisattva's Path to Buddhahood. This is founded on a misunderstanding of the position of a *Buddha* (one who first discovers Dhamma by Enlightenment, exhaustion of the taints), and an *Arahant* (who does the same thing but with the guidelines of the Dhamma which he practises until the exhaustion of the taints occurs). In the Pali Canon, from which all the quotations here are taken, it is clear that the Arahant has reached the final goal. The Buddha sometimes calls all enlightened people *buddha*, those who have woken up.
7. The underlying bases for rebirth are:- The five aggregates, sensual desire, defilements, and kamma.
8. Mahayana (Great Vehicle) Buddhists contrast their own aim - the seeing of all dhammas as empty, with that of 'Hīnayāna' (the Low Vehicle) where the aggregates may be seen as void but not the dhammas. But they do not know perhaps that in the Pali Canon the Buddha himself repeatedly says that dhammas are void, empty, not-self.
9. The name does not imply 'eternal life' which would be only another state of being or existence.
10. The Buddha knew well how men love to speculate on what cannot be put into words. Later Buddhists, called 'Mahayana', fell into the trap of views and even manufactured a Buddhist version of theology. By them the Buddha was conceived of as a phantom, an emanation from an eternal Buddha in a higher sphere (great similarities here to docetic heresies in Christianity). In this and similar Suttas of the Pali Canon the Buddha has pointed out the fruitlessness of such speculations.

Appendix

1

SOME QUESTIONS AND ANSWERS

Q. Please say a few words about the relation of learning to practice of Dhamma in general and meditation in particular.

A. The Buddha was not concerned to propound a philosophical system. His intention is shown in his often repeated words - 'I teach two things only, dukkha and dukkha's cessation.' That is, he taught people how to be able to distinguish their dukkha, how to spot it with mindfulness, and then how to find the path out of dukkha. An eminently practical teaching! His discourses all have this intention - leading people to the lessening and final cessation of dukkha. So learning the Buddha's discourses in the earliest times had only this purpose - as information on the path out of dukkha. Later Buddhists grew more scholastic and were not so much interested in finding this path for themselves but rather in building the Buddha's teaching up into a flawless system which (they hoped) could not be attacked. Much of the Abhidhamma and its commentaries, together with the treatises of Mahayana authors come into this category and from a practical standpoint, especially for meditation, it is all useless. It only clutters the head with more words which, even if they are Dhamma words, have to be put down when meditation starts. Such speculative theories and systems do *not* lead one out of dukkha, nor are they of benefit to others because they cause the dissension which always arises from holding views. By contrast with all this, the Buddha's discourses in Pali point directly to practice on various levels which can only benefit both individuals and society in general. They are words of guidance but they are not to be clung to and have to be put down when meditation starts. The Commentaries rightly depict the Buddha's Teaching as consisting of three stages: thorough learning, practice, and penetration. The first ensures that one has good directions for the journey ahead so that one will not stray off the path. The second is actually walking the path and finding out for oneself the various benefits of virtue, meditation and wisdom. The third is arriving at the goal, the end of the journey, when one completely verifies the Dhamma for oneself. But if one sticks to words and concepts then the second and third parts of the Dhamma cannot be practised and penetrated.

Q. Can one get good advice from a spirit guide or from divination if one has no meditation master to turn to?

A. The Buddha said:

        Oneself is refuge of oneself -

Some Questions and Answers

what else indeed could refuge be?
By the good training of oneself
one gains a refuge hard to gain. (Dhammapada 160)

This means that even when one has a good Teacher he cannot lead one to wisdom, it has to be developed by oneself through the practice of Dhamma. No doubt people do get help in the ways you mention, such as from the Tarot, the 'I Ching' or from astrology but in these ways one's wisdom is not sharpened up because an exterior 'refuge' is being relied on. When Dhamma is practised according to moral conduct, meditation and insight-wisdom then one's heart becomes clearer and brighter so that guidance can be obtained easily from within. Dhamma is then the best path as it is naturally the refuge within one's own mind, speech and body, while the Buddha called such practices as astrology and divination 'the low arts'. Spirit guides or devas cannot be relied upon to give infallible guidance - they are not Enlightened themselves so how could they do this? And besides, they may actually represent, or their messages be coloured by, the subconscious mind of the medium from whom they are obtained. If some evidence is needed of how confused the devas can be a glance at such 'spirit-writings' as the Book of Urantia or the Book of Oahspe should be convincing. These works, supposedly the composition of highly developed spiritual beings show a lamentable ignorance of the Buddha's Teachings, worse indeed than many human beings!

Q. Recently I have had the chance of practising a vipassanā course with a group who say that they alone have the pure way of practice and attainment. What would you say about this?

A. In every religion there are little groups who form sects in time and say that their way is the original pure teaching and everyone else is wrong. But this is just ditthi - views, a way of propping up the ego and has nothing to do with insight! Insight or vipassanā, if it is the real thing, leads to more or less sudden changes in people as their cravings drop off. In groups like the one you mention, have the teachers' cravings dropped off, or are they still attached to a lot of worldly things? And if not to worldly things, then perhaps there is still the attachment to views that 'we have the only true path' and so on? Such are the snares of Mara that he can even lead 'teachers of insight' by the nose! But there is another point in question - vipassanā cannot be practised. One can practise one of the many ways leading to vipassanā (which is not a trade name for one particular group) taught by the many teachers who teach it in Thailand and Burma but the method used cannot be called vipassanā. That is something experienced as a result of the method. Even if one has some unusual experiences they are more likely to arise from calm in the beginning, rather than be concerned with insight. Insight experiences must involve the Three Characteristics, or one of them, and they must have some liberating effect though in the case of 'new' vipassanā this could disappear if not carefully nurtured. Courses are good to take while one has only a limited amount of time but they should not become an addiction! If meditation becomes so important to one's life that one wishes to make it the central theme, then one course after another (with some sensual relapses in between) is not the answer. This lies in the Sangha and renunciation as a monk or nun so that one's lifestyle perfectly fits the way of meditation.

Q. You have told us how important it is to be free from views but in teaching Theravada Buddhism surely you are clinging to those views. Why not give them up?

A. This is an honest and straightforward question. I shall explain it only as far as it is necessary to supplement what has been said elsewhere. (See Chapter IV. 3). Right View - that kamma has appropriate fruits and the Four Noble Truths together do not require that one suspends one's reason and just beliefs. Believing means holding views more or less dogmatically. But in the Dhamma this is not necessary for it is quite easy to test out whether kamma has appropriate fruits or not. Try propping up the bar for a week getting drunk every day and night - and see what kind of results you experience! It is likely that there will be an increase in dukkha! Then compare that week with another spent carefully keeping the Five Precepts and extending loving-kindness and compassion to others. There should be a marked increase of happiness! And this takes no account of the residue of those kammas which may continue fruiting in the future. As to the Four Noble Truths, they do not require belief. They do need understanding though which is then mundane Right View. Afterwards mundane Right View is transformed through insight-wisdom into supermundane Right (Perfect) View which, as has been explained, is No View. The Dhamma I teach is not specially Theravada though I have been trained in this tradition. Dhamma is not Theravada, nor Mahayana either, Dhamma is for putting down views, all views, even Buddhist ones.

Q. I understand from what you have said that your Dhamma-teaching is of the exoteric kind given by the Buddha to his monk disciples who were not mature like the great Bodhisattvas but you have not said much about the practice of esoteric Buddhism suitable for those of an advanced nature. Will you please enlighten us on this?

A. When the Buddha was nearing his Final Nibbana, just before death, he was asked by his attendant Ven. Ananda for his last instructions to the monks. Indian teachers have sometimes left their most closely guarded secrets until a few moments before death before imparting them to a specially favoured disciple. The Buddha, by contrast answered Ven. Ananda in this way: 'I have set forth the Teaching without making any distinction of esoteric and exoteric doctrine; there is nothing with regard to the teachings that the Tathagata holds to the last with the closed fist of a teacher who keeps some things back' - thus indicating that he had no secret teachings which he held back in his 'closed fist'. From other places in the Buddha's discourses, it is clear that he classified those who had religious secrets, such as the brahmins with their Vedas, with rogues and wrongdoers. Why do they hide things? What are they afraid of? - was his attitude to those who held that secrecy and esoteric doctrines were valuable. The Dhamma that he taught, of sila-samadhi-pañña (Moral conduct, meditation and wisdom) was accessible to everyone, not restricted at all for all could question what they did not understand and obtain explanations. It is true that he taught basic Dhamma relating to household duties, good social relationships, virtue and generosity to householders, while monks and nuns received discourses on the deeper aspects of practice, such as detailed descriptions of states of calm and insight and how they could be cultivated. But this does not imply exoteric and esoteric teachings because laypeople when they had developed their practice could hear the same deep Dhamma - nothing was hidden from them. The only way in which they could have any relevance to his teaching is to say 'exoteric' is what one can easily understand while 'esoteric' means what is beyond one's understanding due to delusion and other defilements. But this is not the meaning implied in the question. Though there are now schools of Buddhism which use these terms, the Buddha neither knew of such doctrines nor would he approve of them. Surely these terms imply, on the part of the one who approves them, some kind of 'one-upmanship', a sense of spiritual superiority over those who merely follow 'exoteric doctrines', which must rightly be called pride and conceit. Such thoughts as 'I am a Bodhisattva who follows the esoteric tantric tradition while they have only the exoteric teachings to practise' is only a way of nourishing thoughts of self or ego which cannot result in anything good and cannot be called the practice of Dhamma. Many people are deluded these days because of the prevalence of such terms, mostly in books dealing with Tibetan forms of Buddhism. It may give them a good feeling to follow an 'ear-whispered' tradition with initiations and ceremonies, secret mantras and the promise of magical powers but how far away indeed is all this from what the Buddha taught! That good feeling is just reinforcement of the ego, an obstacle to the attainment of wisdom.

Q. I have studied and practised some Zen and from the little knowledge I have gained it seems that satori is the Zen equivalent of vipassana (insight). Is this correct?

A. It is difficult to compare terms in differing systems of practice but vipassana is clearly defined in the Pali Suttas as being insight into the Three Characteristics of all living beings:- impermanence, dukkha and not-self. If a spiritual experience is not concerned with penetrating these three in oneself then it is not vipassana but rather a samatha calm) experience. So if by satori is meant experiences relating to the Three Characteristics then there is true vipassana in Zen. It is noticeable that Zen Masters do not make much of these three in their instructions, nor do the experiences of their pupils (as related, for instance, in *The Three Pillars of Zen*) reveal penetration of these characteristics. These happenings all seem to be the result of strong calm. So it is evident that satori is a much more loosely defined term than vipassanā, though some satori may qualify to be called insight.

Q. How important is it for a Buddhist to have a guru? I have noticed that you speak about having a Teacher rather than a guru. Is there any difference implied?

A. Yes, it is important for most people. However good a book on meditation may be, it cannot answer one's questions. It is quite common to find that books explain everything about some aspect of meditation *except* the one thing that one needs for guidance. Besides asking a Teacher and being able to get a good reply, the Teacher will on occasion admonish or stir up the disciple if he thinks this necessary. Books can never do this! And one cannot serve a book! But to a Teacher one can show one's reverence and love by such service as is in agreement with the precepts and reasonable. Here is, perhaps, the line which differentiates Buddhist Teachers from Hindu gurus. A Teacher, even if he has reached the peak of Enlightenment, has a natural virtue from which he cannot depart (because there are no defilements to cause this) and he does not expect his disciples to depart from their virtuous conduct in order to serve him. Nor does he want the unreasonable devotion of the blind bhakta. In fact, a Teacher may censure people who get too much concerned with devotion towards him. Devotion should be directed towards Buddha, Dhamma, Sangha and expressed in sincere practice. A Teacher (if a bhikkhu-monk, or bhikkhuni-nun) is a member of the Sangha and not just an individual who teaches how he likes. He has accepted a code of conduct which is common to himself and all other monks. This may be different from a guru too. With the latter, he may speak of 'his grace' in blessing his disciples and frequently a famous guru is identified with one of the Hindu gods; a Buddhist Teacher in the Theravada tradition would never permit this to happen as he is not an incarnation (avatar) or instrument of any divine being, nor does he teach belief in a Creator or any Godhead. The Buddha praised respect to one's Teacher and gratitude for the Teaching he gives:-

> Should one a man of wisdom see
> who points out faults and gives reproof
> as though revealing treasure hid -
> one should consort with such a sage,
> for while one lives with one like him
> better it is, never for worse.
> Let him then exhort, instruct
> and check one from all evil things;
> dear indeed is he to the true
> but to the false he is not dear.
>
> (Dhammapada 76-77)

Q. How can meditation be integrated into ordinary everyday life?

Some Questions and Answers 143.

Doesn't its practice cause one to be inactive in social matters?

A. An answer to the first question is found in Chapter II. 3, the application of mindfulness at first to simple jobs involving the body and later as mindfulness grows stronger, its extension to mindfulness in all situations. This needs patience and perseverance. The second question needs a more detailed answer. Some social matters one should be inactive in and others one should engage in. Those to be avoided are the causes and movements where violence is used or encouraged for the attainment of some goal. From a Buddhist standpoint, *the end never justifies the means.* Violence and hatred can never lead to the attainment of worthy goals. What they do lead to is more violence and hatred. A meditator comes to see this clearly and to know other better non-violent means to deal with injustices and inequalities. For instance, loving-kindness opens many doors which are closed (out of fear) against the violent man. And as meditation develops a clearer mind one knows much better how to approach problems that need to be solved. The answer is clearer and more direct to a successful meditator who does not have a head cluttered up with wandering thoughts and proliferating ideas.

Q. It seems to me to be selfish to go off by yourself and meditate. Surely it would be better to engage in social service. Isn't that what you call the Bodhisattva's work?

A. Bodhisattvas (beings who aspire to Full Enlightenment) must not cultivate only exterior actions of body and speech. If they do only this then how will they differ from the typical western do-gooder? And how can such a person be called a Bodhisattva? Instead of bodhisattvas they will just be body-busies! Bodhi comes from the mind-heart which has been systematically cultivated, not from body and speech actions. The latter when they arise from compassion and a proper sense of duty must not be neglected for they banish selfishness. (Oh, I haven't time to do that, I'm meditating!) But they are not fundamental: mind-heart decides and chooses, mind-heart makes kamma, therefore mind-heart should be properly attended to. Then, if one chooses an active life of good works, that goodness will not lack wisdom and compassion. As regards selfishness, all Buddhist practice to begin with is somewhat selfish because one is rightly concerned with oneself! But the inwardness of meditation which leads to increased purity must be balanced with the growth of loving-kindness and compassion which goes out to all living beings - so the meditator is not selfish but rather finding the way beyond the boundaries of self. *Dhamma can never be practised selfishly*; it always leads to benefit for other beings besides oneself. More Dhamma-practice brings more benefit for beings at large.

Q. You have spoken of crossing yourself over. What about all the many sentient beings? Should one not rather follow the Bodhisattva path and cross them over too?

A. The Buddha's advice to people who have the opportunity to practise Dhamma was they they should practise as much as they possibly could. When Dhamma is practised in the proper way it must benefit both oneself and others. It cannot be practised only to benefit oneself. Giving obviously benefits both sides, the recipient and the donor. Virtue benefits the one who practises Five or Eight Precepts and gives the gift of no-fear to other living beings. Even meditation which seems at first to be an inward-going practice also benefits others because with fewer defilements the meditator relates better to other beings. Mindfulness and meditation must always be complemented by loving-kindness and compassion. This is brought out strongly by the story of Little Fat Pot, the girl acrobat apprentice and her master. (See end of Chapter III.)

The Buddha was once asked by Uttiya, a wanderer, whether the Dhamma provided a way out for all the world, for a half or for a third of it. The Buddha did not reply to this, possibly because the question was phrased in terms of 'beings to be delivered', which is deluded as they are just clung-to aggregates. Venerable Ananda, the Buddha's usual attendant, then gave the simile of a city surrounded by a thick wall having no gaps and only one gate so that the beings entering that place must use the one way in. He goes on to say that entry to the city of Nibbana can only be by way of one gate:
  abandoning the Five Hindrances,
  developing the Seven Enlightenment Factors,
  establishing the mind well in the Four Foundations of Mindfulness.
All beings who wish to enter this city must follow this path to it and enter it in this way.

Perhaps you are thinking of one of the Bodhisattva Vows: 'Though the many beings are numberless, I vow to save them'. This should be seen as an expression of one's loving-kindness towards all beings, it should not be taken literally! Even Gotama the Buddha, or Shakyamuni as he is sometimes called, did not save all *human* beings, what to speak of devas, animals ghosts, and hell-realm beings. Shall I be able to accomplish more than he has done? And if I think that I can, will this not just be conceit? The Sixth Patriarch of Ch'an Buddhism in China has interpreted this vow in an excellent way, fully compatible with the Buddha's original teachings. Here is what he has to say: 'Learned Audience, all of us have now declared that we vow to deliver an infinite number of sentient beings; but what does this mean? It does not mean that I, Hui Neng, am going to deliver them. And who are these sentient beings within our mind? They are the delusive mind, the deceitful mind, the evil mind and suchlike minds - all these are sentient beings. Each of them has to deliver himself by means of his own Essence of Mind. Then the deliverence is genuine.' (Translated by Wong Mou Lam; The Buddhist Society, London) So, saving all beings means saving all the defiled and unwholesome states of mind, for which mindfulness and insight-wisdom will be needed. Just the advice that one might expect from a great Meditation Master!

Another Teacher of practical (as opposed to theoretical) Mahayana, Milarepa the Tibetan yogi, has given similar advice to his disciples. Once they asked him whether they could engage in an active life if it proved beneficial to other beings. He said to them: 'If there is not attachment to selfish aims, you can. But that is difficult. Those who are full of worldly desires can do nothing to help others. They do not even profit themselves. It is as if a man, carried away by a torrent, pretended to save others. Nobody can do anything for sentient beings without first attaining transcendent insight into Reality. Like the blind leading the blind, one would risk being carried away by desires. Because space is limitless and sentient beings innumerable, you will always have a chance to help others when you become capable of doing so. Until then, cultivate the aspiration towards Complete Enlightenment by loving others more than yourselves while practising the Dharma.' (pp.170-171 *The Life of Milarepa*, translated by Lobsang P. Lhalungpa; E.P. Dutton, New York, 1977.).

This is exactly the emphasis of the Buddha in the Pali Canon. There, in the Middle Length Collection, he spoke of a man floundering in a swamp and how he would be unable to help out another - an unenlightened person cannot be the cause of others' enlightenment. Crossed over the ocean of birth and death oneself, one may then help others across effectively.

Q. When you spoke about defilements, you did not mention fear. Why is this? And how can fear be overcome?

A. In Buddhist psychology, the Abhidhamma, fear is not treated as a mental-emotional factor, the reason being that it is a compound of various other things rather than a simple factor. Looked at from the viewpoint of the Five Aggregates fear is a compound of the second, third and fourth: there is always unpleasant *feeling* present; the recognition-identification process with reference to memory of the past which we call *perception* is there; and various *mental formations*, some being kamma resultants while some are fresh kamma, are also to be found. One way out of fear is to analyse it in these terms so as to see that there is not any one thing called fear. Dissolve it away through analysis. Another method is to look at the fear in the light of the Three Roots of Unwholesomeness and find out from which it arises. Usually it will be a compound of all three, greed, aversion and delusion. The last of these must always be present when there is fear since only the ordinary people, the unenlightened, have fear. Fear arises obviously because of clinging to all the conditioned aggregates, sense-bases and elements and trying to regard them as belonging to a self. Contemplation along these lines can sometimes be useful for dispelling fear. The most direct and forceful ways of doing this are only for spiritual heroes such as one finds in the life story of the Venerable Meditation-Master Mun. There, fear of death is overcome by going to live among the remains of the dead, fear of heights by meditating on the edge of a precipice, fear of darkness by meditating at night and by living in a dark cave, and fear of tigers and other wild animals by frequenting the places where they live. Such methods cannot be recommended

Appendix 1

for the less heroic especially when they lack a Teacher. Steady practice of Dhamma in all its aspects, especially daily meditation to strengthen calm, will be very helpful in overcoming fears. But one must not expect any sudden miracles! (See also Chapters VI and VIII).

Q. What about beauty and nature - how can they be used for meditation? I notice that you have spoken of unattractiveness but not of beauty, though in Chinese and Japanese thought, especially Zen, this is much emphasised.

A. Buddhist meditation centres the world over are usually in secluded places which are often very beautiful. However, the aim is undisturbed seclusion rather than the contemplation of a beautiful landscape. Most people who have no spiritual path to follow have some perception of beauty. Unfortunately, this implies that they also have an aversion to the ugly or unattractive. So ordinary people are torn between love for the beautiful and rejection of the ugly. In other words, the first two roots of unwholesomeness, greed and aversion, operate without much restraint in their minds. A meditator has to see that beauty is impermanent and so not be completely attached to it. (Only one who renounces the household life for the homeless state of a monk or nun is likely to have the chance to unwrap all greed and attachment to the beautiful.) He will come to know also that ugly and unattractive things should produce no unhealthy rejection in himself. Beauty and unattractiveness are two sides of the same coin, one is not found without the other. Moreover, both are the work of the discriminating mind and what is beauty to one person is not so to another. While beauty gives a chance for the mind to become attached, unattractiveness used as a contemplation loosens attachment and opens the way to liberation. It is true though, that some people turn to contemplation, even to quite deep and peaceful states, by contemplation of rocks, trees and water. Such meditation cannot proceed further than calm and needs to be augmented by insight, such as the contemplation of impermanence. There are in Theravada, colour-meditations, not dealt with in this book, which are one way of using beauty (see the explanation of *kasinas* in *Path of Purification*, Chapter IV.V). Finally it may be remarked that the Buddha's Final Nibbana took place in exceptionally surroundings, while many of the Arahants of that time uttered verses praising the beauty of the secluded places where they lived. Enlightenment brings a complete appreciation of beauty for there is then no self in the picture to be attached or to want to possess.

Q. You said that imagination is an expression of the root of delusion. What about artistic creativity born of imagination? Do Buddhists regard this as unwholesome?

A. When it is said that imagination is unwholesome this means the sort of distracted mind which is full of past might-have-beens, future may-bes and present fantasies. Such states of mind are useless and point to a lack of mindfulness. Nothing much can be created with this sort of mind, except unwholesome kamma! True artistic creativity is not born of such wandering imagination. More or less of sudden penetrating clarity is needed (according to the artform used) combined with greater or lesser perseverance in executing the work. Both the clarity, a kind of aesthetic insight, and the perseverance, which implies mindfulness and full awareness are wholesome mental-emotional factors. While the creation of artistic works in this way cannot supersede meditation it can complement it to a great degree. The master artists that the Buddhist world has produced, (all anonymous, perhaps the influence of the not-self teaching), such as those that produced the murals of Ajanta - done on wet plaster so that lines could not be changed, or Ch'an/Zen artists in China and Japan where a similar principle applied, or the sculptors of sublimely peaceful Buddha-images such as those found in Sri Lanka, all of them needed intense mindfulness and concentration, combined no doubt with that happy and peculiarly Buddhist lack of 'seriousness' which gives all their creations a freedom and spontaneity, the marvellous half-smile on the Buddha's lips.

Appendix

2

A GLOSSARY OF BUDDHIST TECHNICAL TERMS ON MEDITATION

All words are given first in their Pāli form, followed by the Sanskrit (S) and the Modern Thai pronunciation (T) where these differ from Pāli.

akusala (akuśala (S), akuson (T)), *unwholesome*. All acts (kammas) of mind, speech and body which are rooted in the Three Roots of Unwholesomeness: greed, aversion and delusion.

arahant (arhat (S), pra arahang (T)), *one of supreme worth*. Enlightened by fully penetrating the Dhamma and thereby cutting off all defilements and obstructions.

ariya (ārya (S), pra ariya (T)), *noble one*. Those who have partly or wholly penetrated Dhamma in themselves. Includes stream-winners, once-returners, non-returners and arahants.

āsava (āśrava (S)), *taints*. The deepest level of distortion in the mind. Three or four taints are described:- the taint of sensuality, the taint of being (existence, becoming), the taint of ignorance; the taint of views is sometimes added.

bhāvanā, *development*. Two sorts:- the development of calm and of insight. The word means literally 'making become'.

citta (chit, chit-chai (T)), *mind-heart*. That which knows, or is conscious. A word that encompasses the many changing processes both intellectual and emotional.

dukkha (dukkha (S) tukh (T)), *unsatisfactoriness, suffering*, whether gross or subtle, physical or mental, just being (I am) in the round of birth and death - all this is dukkha. This does *not* mean that the Buddha taught 'All life is suffering'!

ekaggatā (ekagratā (S)), *one-pointedness, singleness of mind*. The pure concentrated mind that dwells continuously on one meditation subject wordlessly.

jhāna (dhyāna (S), chān (T)), deep concentration. A nearly effortless absorption in the meditation subject when there is no sense-awareness at all but calm, purity and mindfulness in the heart.

kammatṭāna (karmasthāna (S), kammathān (T)), literally 'work-place', the *meditation subject* with which the mind is occupied, such as mindfulness of breathing, or loving-kindness.

kilesa (kleśa (S), kilet (T)), *defilement*. That which makes the mind dirty, such as anger, lust, boredom etc. The mental-emotional factors on which are built unwholesome states of mind.

kusala (kuśala (S), kuson (T)), *wholesome*. Every mental state rooted in non-greed, non-aversion, non-delusion - the Three Roots of Wholesomeness, and the acts of body and speech dependent on them.

magga (marga (S), magg (T)), *path*. The Path moments of Stream-winner and so on up to Arahant when one sees Nibbana, becomes a Noble One (ariya) and *is* the Noble Eightfold Path.

māra (man (T)), literally *the destroyer*. Evil objectified and sometimes personified. Objectified as defilements (*kilesa*), the five grasped-at aggregates, kamma, and death. Personified as the lord of the realm of sensuality, a deva who wishes to keep all beings in the round of rebirth.

paññā (prajñā (S)), *wisdom*. In its highest meaning, the penetrative insight into the Three Characteristics of existence which leads to Enlightenment. Ability to distinguish unwholesome actions from wholesome ones, a clear memory, the intellect applied to wholesome things and the lesser insights (vipassanā) are also included.

patipatti (pratipatti (S), batibat (T)), *practice*. Not only the practice of formal meditation but of the whole Dhamma of sīla-samādhi-paññā.

phala (phon (T)), *fruit*. The Fruit moments follow the Path-moments and in the case of the first three paths last only a short time. In the case of the Arahant, the fruit is a meditative state of jhana which can be enjoyed at any time.

pīti (prīti (S)), *rapture*. Varying degrees of stimulation in the body, usually pleasant but not always so, which grow stronger towards jhāna but is abandoned on entering the third jhana.

puthujjana (prthagjana (S), puthujon (T)), *ordinary person*. One who has not yet seen at least Stream-winning and so is not an Ariya or Noble One.

samādhi, collectedness. A collective name for various deep meditative states such as the jhānas.

samatha, calm. Usually the first result of practising meditation. Some methods lead only to this and do not follow on to insight or vipassanā.

Appendix 2

saṁyojana, fetter. The ten fetters have been outlined in the last chapter.

sati (smrti (S)), *mindfulness,* sometimes also *memory.* Awareness of the actions and state of mind and body here and now. A moderate amount is equivalent to normality or sanity.

satipatthāna, (smrtyupasthāna (S), satipathān (T)), *the foundations of mindfulness.* Under the four headings of body, feeling, mental states, and mental factors, are given various exercises for promoting the growth of mindfulness.

sīla (śīla (S), sīn (T)), *virtue, moral conduct, the precepts.* These are outlined in such formulations as the Five Precepts for lay people generally, the Eight for special occasions as when they meditate, the Ten for novices, the 227 for monks and the 311 for nuns.

sukha, (suk (T)), *happiness* - may be derived from material things which are conditioned, so the happiness arising dependent on them is impermanent, or from non-material actions such as practising any aspect of Dhamma - a happiness which is more secure but still not eternal. The highest Happiness is Nibbana, the Unconditioned Element which is unchanging.

vipassanā, (vidarśana (S)), *insight.* The seeing in oneself of the Three Characteristics in the five aggregates so that clinging is cut off.

INDEX

Aggregates, Five, 42f, 70, 127
Agitation and worry, 54
Anger, 76ff
Arahant, 126ff
Artistic creativity, 146
Aversion, 22
Awareness, Full, 32f

Beauty, 146
Believing, 12
Black magic, 115
Bliss, 58
Bodhisatta, 80f, 143ff
Body, 6ff
Body, Contemplation of, 29ff
Breathing, mindfulness of, 30f, 92ff
Buddha, Recollection of, 100ff
Buddha, Refuge in, 13ff

Calm, Development of, 52ff
Cessation, 46
Characteristics, Three, 67ff
Clinging, 73
Commercialism, 116
Compassion, 40
Conceit, 71, 116ff, 127
Conditioned things, 67f
Contemplation, 29ff
Craving, 45f

Defilements, 21ff
Delusion, 22
Dhamma, as Refuge, 15ff
Dhammas, 72
Dreams, 119f
Dukkha, 44f, 69

Effort, Right, 23ff
Emotion, 34ff
Enlightment, Seven Factors of, 43f
Esoteric, 140

Fantasies, 119
Faults of others, 78
Fear, 89, 107ff, 119, 145

Feeling, Contemplation of, 34ff
Fetters, Ten, 125f
Food, 7f
Forgiveness, 77
Formless Concentrations, 60
Friends, 1ff

Generósity, 38
Gentleness, 75f
Giving, 82
God, 14, 17, 61, 114, 131
Going for Refuge, 13ff
Greed, 21
Guru, 142

Heart of the Buddha's Teachings, 64
Helpfulness, 77
Hindrances, Five, 41f, 52ff
Ill-will, 53
Impermanence, 68f
Initial Application, 57
Insight, 62ff, 118
Insight, Development of, 67
Intolerance, 109

Jhana, 56ff

Kamma, 80
Kundalini, 110

Learning and Practice, 138
Lethargy and Drowsiness, 53
Liberation of the heart, 60
Loving-kindness, 39ff, 75ff, 105f
Loving-kindness, Discourse on, 85f

Magic, 114
Mantra, 63
Meditation subjects, 75ff, 109f
Mental Events, Contemplation of, 41ff
Mental States, Contemplation of, 36ff
Mind, 20ff

Index

Mindfulness, Daily, 26ff
Mindfulness, Four Foundations of, 29ff
Motivation, 113

Neighbourhood Concentration, 56
Nibbana, 122, 130f
Noble Eightfold Path, 47, 130
Noble Ones, 123
Noble Sangha, 123
Noble Truths, 44ff, 66
Non-aversion, 39ff
Non-delusion, 40ff
Non-greed, 38ff, 46
Non-returner, 125f
Not self, 70f, 131

Occult, 114
Once-returner, 125
One-pointedness, 58
Ordinary people, 130

Posture, 9f
Postures, Four, 31f
Power, 114
Preacher of Patience, 80f
Precepts, Five and Eight, 4ff, 113
Progress, 105

Rapture, 57, 110
Recollections of Three Jewels, 108f
Refuges, 11ff
Renunciation, 38
Right View, 66f
Roots, Three, of Unwholesomeness, 21ff, 129
Roots, Three, of Wholesomeness, 38ff

Sangha, as Refuge, 16f
Satori, 141
Sceptical Doubt, 54
  Selfishness and meditation, 143
Selflessness, 38
Self-theory, 73
Sensual Desire, 52
Sex, 5, 6, 116

Shame and Fear of Blame, 110, 116
Social affairs, 143
Soul, 61, 131
Spirits, 115, 138f
Spiritual Faculties, Five, 50ff
Stream-entry, 123ff
Surroundings, 3f
Sustained Application, 57

Taints, Three, 128f
Tantricism, 115f
Tathagata, conceiving about, 133ff
Teacher, 142
Trance, 55

Unattractive, Perception of, 96ff
Unwholesome, 21ff

Views, 64ff, 71, 109, 139f, 140
Virtue, 4ff, 113
Visions, 105, 106f
Void, 72, 131ff

Walking Meditation, 94ff
Wisdom, 40

Yoga, 6ff

Zen, 141f

Printed in Great Britain by
Amazon.co.uk, Ltd.,
Marston Gate.